CW00382629

22.2.2020

To an amazing Queen Andrya

Soul

A

Woman

A Journey to Self Love

Neusa Catoja

Thank you for our beautiful connection. May this book remind you of your worth. From self love to self love. You are enough.

Luv Neusa x

Soul of A Woman

Soul of A Woman

Published in London by Peaches Publications, 2020.

www.peachespublications.co.uk

The moral right of the author has been asserted.

British Library Cataloguing in Publication Data: A catalogue record for this book is available from the British Library.

ISBN: 9798609989772

Book cover jacket design: Peaches Publications.

Typesetter: Winsome Duncan.

Proofreader: Tamara Georgeou.

Soul of A Woman

Disclaimer

The contents of this book are for informational purposes only. The content is not intended to be a substitute for professional advice, diagnosis, or treatment. Always seek the advice of your mental health professional or other qualified health provider with any questions you may have regarding your condition. Never disregard professional advice or delay in seeking it because of something you have read in this book.

If you are already seeking medical advice. Please continue to do so and inform your GP/medical professional of any changes you wish to make and seek their guidance whilst using this book to support and guide your journey to mental, physical and emotional wellbeing.

If you are in crisis and don't feel you can keep yourself safe right now, seek immediate help:

- Go to any **Accident & Emergency (A&E) department.**
- Call 999 and ask for an ambulance to take you to A&E.
- Ask someone else to call 999 for you or take you to A&E.

If you need urgent support but don't want to go to A&E, you could:

- call Samaritans on freephone 116 123 – they're always open and are there to listen
- contact your GP surgery and ask for an emergency appointment
- contact NHS 111 (England) or NHS Direct 0845 46 47 (Wales)
- contact your local crisis team (CRHT), if you're under their care

Soul of A Woman

Contents

Dedication

I dedicate this book to two women. My two Mothers. Family unity, faith and love are their biggest values which were passed onto us all.

My Biological Mother (Mãe) Zelia dos Anjos Fonseca, Anjos, meaning Angel in Portuguese. She is my Angel. The one, who never doubted me, never left me and never gave up on me. She taught me everything I needed to know to be the Great woman that I am today.

Obrigada Mãe, my best friend, my father, my role model, my everything. When I felt lost at times and questioned who I am I looked at you for strength. In all the suffering you went through, I never saw you shed a tear. I had become a reflection of you...

You are A Queen

I wish You saw Your Worth as a Woman
I wish You believed that You deserve to be Loved
I wish You would see that You are my Hero and my Strength
I wish You would allow Yourself to be taken care of
I wish You could see how beautiful You are
I wish You would release Your painful past
I wish You would stop worrying about others
I wish You would be Selfless and Live Life more
I wish You saw Yourself as the Queen that You are
Strong, Resilient, Worthy, Loving, Caring, Unique, at times
crazy and oh so Beautiful

*'When I was young, I used to stare at you putting on your
makeup, with so much Love. In that moment I knew I was
never alone, you are more than just a Mother,
You are my Angel'*

My chosen Mother, who sadly left us, Maureen Bourne. We
hadn't seen each other for years. Yet God made it so that we
had our final meeting. We talked about the good times: your
angelic voice and words, expressing how much you loved your
children, gave birth to the name of this book. As I left you, it's
like we'd never been apart. I sat on the train, let out a
satisfying yet sad smile, put pen to paper and Soul of A
Woman poem was birthed...

Soul of A Woman

In Her eyes Life had been
Breathing slowly to Her Sweet Symphony
Ever changing in Her Essence
Ever present in Her silence
She lived life Freely
Her family Her biggest Value
Her fuel
Her core
The Love She gave
Is what She Lived for
She never lost
Yet always gained
So much more than what She had
Where She is going is not to make You sad
She Lived and did all that She could
Never what they said or what She should
Her stubbornness often misunderstood for selfishness
Don't tell Her what is best for Her
Even in Her resting place
Think before You say it just in case
You're not prepared for what She will say
Leave Her to be still and Pray
Her voice spoken in sweet whispers
Yet Her gaze lingers
On Your actions
Your every word
'I Love You my child, You don't know just how much I do' She
lovingly utters with a smile and a warm tear
*'You don't have to be strong all the time, just remember I'm
within You'*
I'm at peace now
The storm is over
I came to fulfil my mission
And leave a vision
That You can now clearly see

Soul of A Woman

It's time for You to be Free
'You've loved me so much'
'Now it's time for You to allow Yourself to receive that love'
My part is done
My mission accomplished
In physical presence it's time for me to go
However just remember I'm still here in the Spiritual realm
I can never leave You
Or be forgotten
I live inside of all of You
If You ever feel sad
Put on my favourite soca jam
'Now go on bad'
Laugh at this image
Laugh at the good times that we had
Just remember to pass on my legacy
To Live Laugh
And most importantly
Spread Love

*Dedicated to a beautiful loving Mother. She lived purposely,
laughed unapologetically and loved unconditionally.*

RIP My Queen 10.12.19

Acknowledgements

I would like to express my deepest gratitude to the person that made the production of this book possible. My Publisher, Winsome Duncan, from Peaches Publications. At our first encounter we both opened up about our own struggles: a connection, with one vision: to speak up and help others, was visible. I knew right there and then that I was no longer going to self-publish this book. If I was going to show the world my talent and heal others I had to do it with the right guidance and love, and this lady showed it from the start. I still love to call you *'Peaches'*. Thank you, my beautiful sister, for giving me so much insight before we even started working together, guiding me through this whole process. We always gave each other food for thought, and wow, we never had quick conversations on the phone; even though we always started off with saying *'Just a quick one'*. From the moment I said *'Yes, you are the one'* it became so. Man, there was so much resistance, tears, pain and many drafts. I tried to hold onto my story, but I knew there was only one thing holding me back from being that butterfly that flows so effortlessly, to unleash this book, my truth, the real rawness of how I rose up again, from the ashes of my own burnt-out, exhausted body and drowning in my own tears. Love you girl for inspiring me to let it go. I am super excited at how loud we are going to roar with our voices through our books and public speaking engagements. I know this book is only the beginning.

These next few thank you's were written as I celebrated my 40th Birthday. However, as I wrote, I soaked my journal with tears. My makeup looked so good I didn't want to spoil it, and so kept them for the right moment: and now this is the moment.

Thank you all for being here at what I call my *'Bestest most Transformational Year'*. The Year I said *'YES I am Worthy'* of all the Love and laughter we have shared, and will continue to share, even when I felt the Love for myself had disappeared.

Still, you all remained, wondering why I had become so distant, why I couldn't get up and rise like I used to. The truth is I thought I had to have it all under control and *'Be Perfect'* because that's what I thought you all expected of me. I thought that only I could make myself better, and that no one would understand me, how could you when I couldn't understand *'it'* myself.

I chose not to be a burden, that's why my fall came so suddenly. It was a message from God, reminding me of all the Love that each one of you had, and still always have, for me; and that in my own loneliness you still believed I would set myself Free.

Dear Mãe, it was your Faith in me when you often said *'Filha Tu Vais Vencer' (daughter you will overcome)*. Your strength and resilience as a beautiful loving woman created this very stubborn yet loving woman that I am today. I am a reflection of You. I always said you are my *'Best friend'* and in those moments when I used to avoid your phone calls, you always appeared in presence to Love and nurture me. I Love you endlessly, unconditionally and spiritually, Mãe.

Sister Ema, it was your crazy, sexy, cool ways that kept me laughing when I couldn't smile. Remember the day you put on Tina Turner's *'Proud Mary and Rolling on the River'* and made me dance like a crazy woman until we exhausted ourselves. Your madness is unlike any other. I Love your stupid smile and your beautiful face. *'Don't ever change'*.

Brother Arnaldo (aka Neil), I remember when you phoned me and said *'Sis all you need is a good man to take care of your needs'* and that you would help me find one, boy did I not want to have that conversation with you, not then, and not now. But you were right, I found him and yes your advice was right. *'Be you Bruv'* and inspire others to be themselves. Mãe placed a seed inside us all, that's why we were born a day apart. We were meant to be twins and you know what *'Love resides in you'*, where there is love there is no room for hate. Use this Love to take your thoughts and life to a peaceful place. Take the driver's seat and take the passengers that you love along this ride with you. *'You are a true King'*.

Brother Joao. We may be distant in space, but never in time. Your silence means your cave is where you feel safe. You have created the family unit Mãe taught us. However this family unit has space to grow and include all of those who still love and care for you. Make a change, bring Love where resentment lives. *'You have the seed'*.

Goddaughter and cousin, Catia, I remember the time you cooked and cleaned my house and told me how beautiful I still looked, even though I didn't see it, with no judgement, your compliments were continuous. You have broken the chain, *'be proud and believe in you'*. Thank you for always saying that I am your role model, here is something that you don't know *'I admire you too'*.

My beautiful cousin Nadia, my twin. Your strength and ability to get up despite your own challenges in life made me question the strength within me. If I am your twin I knew I'd one day break free. You're resilience is that of a true *Hustler*. God is blessing you for all that you have been through. *'Love lives within You'*.

Soul of A Woman

Tia Melita, my dear Auntie, you always told everyone to leave me alone, often saying *'Shhhh stop that nonsense, 'She's fine'.* Thank you for being my other Mother and for all your *'Good morning messages'. 'That fire you hold is within me'. Be proud Tia, there are no rights or wrongs in life, we all do the best we can'.*

Dionne, my sister in law, the many conversations we had that showed how much you cared and you always told me about the prayers you and my niece Khalisah always said for me, Ending the call with *'Inshallah'.* Your prayers were answered.

The rest of my very big family, here in London and spread across Portugal and Mozambique. I love you all, our paths will cross very soon.

My P.U.T.A.S. aka (Professional, Unique, Talented, Amazing Sisters), life, even when dark, your friendship was consistent, your compassion was amazing, and you always had time for me, to my Caribbean and African Queens, thank you all for being my truest sisters from another Mister and blessing me with the maddest, most wildest times. Bestie Dominique we've been through thick and thin but we always said we would always have each other's back no matter what. We've both fallen hard, now it's time to *'Rise Again', 'Putas till the end'.*

My baby girl, Jaida-Phoenix, You saved me. At times it got too much, but I always looked forward to hearing you sing. At times I'd be so low, you just sang, your sweet voice touched me and reminded me that I created the most amazing, smart, creative, talented, strong, beautiful Queen. Even though sometimes we get on each other's nerves, you are my greatest creation and because of you I had to get up, to be an example that when life gets tough we must be true to ourselves and create our own happiness. *'Dream, Believe, Achieve'*.

A sincere note of Gratitude to my Spiritual sister and Diamond Queen Henriette Djedou. Founder of Diamond Ecoute, for hearing my fall in December 2016; listening to my rise in April 2018; and providing the stage for me to share my story. Embracing the Diamond Within gave birth to a Public Speaker. I had no idea I had this gift inside me, you guided me to unleash it. *'Keep helping the world around you, the world needs more people like you'*.

Hannah Kupoluyi, founder of All Women's Network, You, my sister, are a Queen. You opened the door for me to use my voice around other amazing women in business. There are no limits to what you create. You are God's Angel and I am super excited to see your beautiful face as you continue to shine bright with so much grace. *'God placed a seed that is constantly growing and being passed on, keep watering it'*.

I cannot stop until I give a massive thank you to my Inspiration, my friend, my sister, and my burpee Queen Maydinne Etienne-Thomas. You inspired me to become a fitness professional. Your energy, your hardcore movement is addictive yet your laughter is contagious. You reminded me to stay true to myself, encouraging me to never give up on my dreams when I began to lose myself and now you continue to Inspire me with the *'Live, Laugh and Spread love'* messages. I love seeing your daily videos and being energised by your presence. Love you and Kenny Ken my extended family. *'Never ever ever stop sharing your love'*. Here is a poem I once shared when you posted a beautiful picture of you...

She is a Queen

My Inspiration
She is Her own reflection
What You see is Beauty
A Queen of Love
A Creator of Her own Destiny
Her Smile is infectious
Her Laugh is contagious
Her Strength is a result of Her own Vulnerability
She Hides nothing
Yet She gives Everything
Don't take Her Kindness for granted
Just remember She is the *'Burpee Queen'*
If that doesn't scare You
Or intimidate You
Then let Her *'Terminator'* terminate You
She simply is what Life should be
Live Laugh Love
Her Energy will set You Free
She is like You
She is like Me
She is a Diamond
She is simply *'May May'*
My Sister
My Friend
My message that always reminds Me
To be Me
I LOVE LOVE LOVE the reflection staring back with Admiration
She really is so much more than what Your eyes can see

Love You my Queen and thank You for sharing Your best memories, stories, wisdom, guidance and friendship with me.

Dionne Williams, founder of GetsetLondon, my amazing Coach and Asari St Hill my Actioncoach. Yes it takes a team to support a Vision and help it grow. It also takes a push to make this Queen listen. You both have, and continue, to push me past my boundaries to unleash all the magic inside. Thank you for what you have helped to ignite: the light that keeps forever burning with ideas and excitement. *'Business is so much fun with You both guiding me. Every great Coach needs a greater Coach'.*

Last, but definitely not least, Simon, my partner in crime. My sexy man, my friend, my twin flame. You saw my descend, you showed me what true friendship means, you saw my rise and showed me what pure Love means. You encourage me, support me, challenge me and Love me like no other. I finally began to know what it feels like to be accepted and Loved for simply being me, at my worst you never let me go. You always used to say, *'You are God'* I never knew what you meant until the day I connected Spiritually. I finally understood that God was always inside me. I just needed to Believe and search within. I am so looking forward to the memories we continue to create. *'Your Loving is my magic pill'.*

'Family are those we are born into however a 'Family Unit' comes from the roots and ingredients we continuously put into making the Family Loving and united. I chose You all, never by coincidence. I chose You all because God made it so'.

It's been a hard and long rollercoaster ride, one that I would not change even if I could. It taught me many lessons but in all the darkness I learnt what you have all taught me:

That the Love you give to me I must first give to myself and as I do I am able to pour it into each and everyone of you. You taught me that I am the most important person in my life.

Some of you just give tough Love, you know who you are.

I want to thank you all for being a Loving presence in my life and the reason I am alive. Thank you.

Foreword

By Dionne Williams

Neusa has the amazing ability to describe waves of deep, emotional pain, as well as joy, in a way that you can't help but feel deeply on an internal level.

This is why it's always so easy to connect to Her authenticity; through Her words and the way you are guided towards questioning your own personal internal narrative, that controls your actions and behaviours. It also makes reading this book likely to touch your heart in ways that are both warming and wrenching at the same time.

Having had the pleasure of coaching Neusa and getting to know Her on a very personal level, it is obvious that She really does have a gift of effortlessly articulating Her thoughts and experiences in a way that you can't help but feel moved, inspired and opened by, more so than you were before reading or listening to Her words.

The simple exercises and tips provided throughout this book are going to open up your ability to see yourself in an entirely more Loving and powerful way, as you read and reflect on Her words. Throughout, Neusa is guiding you, supporting you and leading the way, through Her writing and thought-provoking questioning, to a happier, healthier and empowered state of being.

Neusa beautifully expresses so much of what many women would Love to be given: , an opportunity to share Her Soul, in this beautiful, what will soon be your go-to guide to filling yourself up with Love, inspiration and a belief in your own innate ability to rise after going through what is labelled as depression, book.

Get comfortable, grab a pen and paper, meditate on the exercises, and enjoy.

The Beginning

It was the summer of 2015
Warm with a summer breeze
Birds singing so sweetly
Flowers creating beauty upon trees
Wedding bells surrounded by smiles
The bride excited yet nervous to say *'YES'* to Her King
One should feel blessed to be awake
Grateful to witness this day
Yet life had stolen Her beautiful smile
Hidden in endless pain permanently yet only for awhile
Look into Her eyes
Lifeless
Distant
Stuck restless mind
Trapped
Disconnected
Full of guilt
Hatred
Shame
Regret
Makeup became Her *"make up"*
She hid Her flaws behind the paint
The tiredness
The fake smile
The *'Yes I am ok'*
Wanting to scream so loud *'No I feel like I'm dead'*
Speechless yet so many things She wanted to express
Shouting louder
Yet silenced in Her words
'It's ok this struggle has a purpose'
'It's ok just keep your head above the surface'
'Soon your smile will light up the world'
Until that day *'just pretend'*
Wait patiently
Soon Your story will be told...

The Diagnosis

The day has come to hear my fate
Better do it now before it's too late
Anxiously waiting for expert advice
They know better
They are wise
Wise enough to know why this is happening
They studied
Seen many others
They have experience
They will send me for scanning
Brain on overload
Thousands of thoughts
Lots of stories untold
Waiting for the tests
The questions
The diagnosis
'It will go away once and for all'
'Soon I will be standing 5.5inches tall'
Doubts worry fear
Calmness exhaustive tear
Soon there will be nothing here
Just a body that's existing
A mind that has no giving
I enter the room
'Fake it till You make it smile'
Even if it feels so gloom
Disconnected physically
Present yet distant
Stuck in the past
'How long will this feeling last'
'What can I do for You?' He says
Uninterested rushing me through His 6 minute consultation time
'I'm not sleeping and feel quite on edge' I nervously whisper

Soul of A Woman

'Well here is a pill'
'Take it everyday'
'What will it help me with Doctor?' I say
'It's to help with "YOUR DEPRESSION" He confidently affirms
My heart beats
Hands sweaty
Mind racing
'What When How' Breathhhhhhhhhhe
'Me DEPRESSED NO WAY'
'I am fit young strong healthy, even if I don't feel myself lately'
'Is He sure'
'Is there a test to double check'
He looks at me for the first time with sympathy
'It will take 6-8 weeks for any effect to take place'
'Come and see me then' He affirms with empathy
'HOLD ON WAIT'
'I CAN'T BREATHE'
'I AM DEPRESSED'

'As You speak so shall You Become'

Dr Wayne Dyer

The Breakdown

When a seed is planted it can only grow by what you feed it and the attention you give it. The Doctor had planted the seed that I was *"Depressed"* it formed a belief for my symptoms. A seed I had never had before. I'd heard of depression many times. People often refer to it as *'I felt depressed yesterday'* *'I'm depressed because I didn't get paid', I'm depressed because I broke up with my partner'* etc. So this is what I knew about depression. Yet I didn't just feel down, I felt uneasy, like someone had placed something in my stomach that tightened every time I wanted to move. A heavy weight was placed on my shoulders and my head wouldn't stop jumping from thought to thought. I began to walk around with a heavy fog like cloud, no matter what time of day it was. I was a Personal Trainer with a busy client base, teaching classes, inspiring others; I had an amazing body and trained 6 days a week. I was eating the right amount of food for the training I was doing. I had a goal to become a Fitness Model and enter my first competition *'Miami Pro'*. I had a plan for training and nutrition, I was self-employed and earning more money than I had ever earned. I was single so had no stress from a relationship. I had an amazing supportive family, friends, a daughter I was much closed to and loved, who was about to start secondary school. So how can this just happen?

I didn't want to accept what he said. Yet the words played in my mind constantly. I started to nurture and grow the very seed I did not want to accept I had.

I looked at the white box with green writing clearly labelled *'Citalopram'*, alongside my name. Instructions to take one a day, everyday. I opened the box upon a friend's advice I took one because She said they helped Her and it would help me too. I didn't believe that it would help me, but I felt helpless, exhausted, so I took it, went to lie down, sleep never came. My mind was racing. *'I have failed', 'I am depressed'*. My Mind entered a daze I cannot explain.

Reflection

Every thought, every action, becomes a belief forming habit that either causes growth or death, keeping you stuck in a vicious cycle.

I was now labelled *"DEPRESSED"*. So I played that role without accepting it, yet I lived like a depressed person. I allowed negativity to live in my Mind.

I went to the Doctor for help, yet I didn't want his help. Deep down I knew I had the remedy. I remember telling my best friend *'I don't believe this pill will fix me'*. She affirmed time and time again, *'I know it won't because you don't believe it will'*.

You see again it came down to me again. *'It's all my fault nothing works' 'It's my fault I'm depressed' 'SOMEBODY HELP ME PLEASE!' 'I CAN'T SHAKE THIS FEELING OFF!'*.

What came over the next few weeks from *"Affirming" 'I Am DEPRESSED'* to *"Believing"* that a pill won't fix me, came the *"Actions"* that supported my *"Thoughts"*.

Little did I know that my symptoms were a result of what I thought was a *"Healthy Bodybuilders Diet"*. The word itself means *"Die"*. It became an obsession for me, the pursuit of the *"PERFECT BODY"*.

Who comes to steal your joy but a thief in the night? It comes when there is darkness as we give way to self-destruction. *'Thoughts become things'*. Have you ever thought about someone you haven't seen in ages and you either bump into them, they text you or call? Or how many times have you wanted a red dress, or a silver car and you keep seeing that same colour dress or silver car and no matter what, it appears in your existence?

It's the power of thought. What you think...Hold that thought for 17 seconds and boom it manifests?

Do you not now see the correlation between your thoughts and your reality?

The realisation that I was not *"DEPRESSED"* only came to me in 2017. When I finally listened intuitively: my Mind needed *"Rest"*; My Body needed *"Nourishment"*. Back then I didn't listen. Instead I continued pushing through and trying to fix me externally. I wanted so badly to feel better now. So my dieting obsession began and I became fixated on *"fixing me"*.

Exercise 1

Begin to be mindful of the thoughts you are having. The constant internal dialogue, the conversations and thoughts playing around in your head. Are they good thoughts that energise you or low vibrational thoughts that deplete you?

Did you know that the Mind gets rapidly exhausted when it's constantly battling with negative thoughts?

Exercise 2

Answer the following questions as honestly as possible, *YES* OR *NO*.

Do you know how to switch negative thoughts off?
Do you believe the thoughts are true?
Are they becoming your everyday Mantra?
Are they affecting your life?
Are they keeping you stuck?
Would you repeat these words to your loved ones?

If you answered 'yes' to most of these questions and desire to change, take action below. Let's challenge these thoughts.

Look back at your answers.
Do they surprise you, shock you or cause you to feel anxious?

Exercise 3

Let's put pen to paper and I call it vomit,

because it's like a brain dump of something toxic.

Get your Journal out. Write down all of your thoughts that you can remember from the day, or just what comes up. The best time of the day to do this is first thing in the morning when the mind is very active, or before sleep as the Mind is restless. On the left side, put all the negative/unwanted thoughts. On the right side, put all the positive/manifesting thoughts. Read the left, then read the right.

Now go back to your journal and look at the list of the negative thoughts and see what you are constantly manifesting into your existence.

I am about to tell you something very important: that once you get this concept you will start to become very mindful of your internal language, and your actions to make that thought into reality.

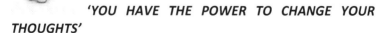

'YOU HAVE THE POWER TO CHANGE YOUR THOUGHTS'

The laws of attraction are just that. What you think, you begin to attract. From attraction, it's the belief that becomes the first ingredient, then to make that thought a reality we take action in bringing it into existence, first by speaking it and it manifests into the presence of the very thing that we don't want or want?

'WHAT YOU FOCUS ON YOU ATTRACT'

So in order to get what we want we must first:

1. *THINK of something we want*

2. *HOLD IT FOR 17 SECONDS*

3. *BELIEVE IN THE POWER OF MANIFESTATION*

4. *Take Action because we already believe in it, so when we*

Act, it becomes our Reality.

"You Become what You Focus on"

What's Happening

Struggling mentally
Physically exhausted
Anxiously hoping
Praying faithfully
My mind is not my own
This tired ugly body feels so drained
So weary
So alone
'I'm so afraid I'll lose control'
This world is so big so why does it feel so small
Worry causes anxiety
Anxiety causes fears
Fear causes pain
Pain causes worry
Worry causes frustration
Self-fulfilling condemnation
Frustration causes anger
Anger causes self-harm
Self-harm causes *DANGER*
[Deep breath]
If I am bringing worry
Then I Am the cause
The cause of all this mess
The reason for all this stress
If I can just go back
And focus on the cause
Then I can stop this anxious feeling
From growing right under my nose
[Deep satisfying breath]
There really is nothing wrong with Me
I Am not mentally ill
Like my Psychiatrist said
I do not need a pill to fix this burning breath
I Am just a side effect of the suppression of my Spiritual Being

Soul of A Woman

That craves for Love
Craves for a purpose
A meaning to this thing called *"Life"*
A Being that wants to be still
A Mind that wants to be calm
A purpose that wants to be fulfilled
A true high vibrational Spirit that wants to be FREE

"Don't strive to understand it all, take one step forward and let Your story unfold"

As I think, so Shall I Become

Brave
Bold
Independent
Beautiful
Sexy
Caring
Loving
Kind
Unique
These were the words that described Me internally
Healthy
Soft curly hair
Brown skin
Big brown eyes
Big African pouting lips
Tiny pert breasts
Wide strong shoulders
Flat abs
Sexy strong curvaceous thighs
Big bootylicious behind
I once prided myself for having a *"5 Star Physique"*
These were the words that described who I was externally
These words do not define Me
Yet they consumed Me
Confidence was a trait that I wore effortlessly
Wise was a gift that I had subconsciously
I became who my Mind said I was
I lived life mindlessly just because
No one taught me that my thoughts had become a part of Me
'Life or Death are in the Power of the tongue' Proverbs 18:21
No one knew how I did things so quickly and selflessly
Only my Mind knew Me so
Exquisitely
A seed when planted can grow to bear fruits and flowers so
beautifully

Soul of A Woman

You plant it
Nourish it
Shine it with light
Love it with kind words
You also kill it with darkness
Neglect
Hate with horrible thoughts
As I think so shall I be
Confused
Frustrated
Abusive
Hateful
Shame
Guilt
Blame
Dark destructive thoughts
Came to Steal
Kill and Destroy
It came to stop me from unleashing the *"Greatness"* within
Me

"If You change the way You look at things, the things You look at change."

Dr Wayne Dyer

Be Bold

I am the Beauty that lies within
I am the Diamond You cannot see
I love so deep and unconditionally
I give my all so passionately
Behind the laughter
Lies a sadness that keeps appearing mindlessly
Bringing back to a place so familiar to me
It's like an anchor so vivid
So alive so close
I clench my teeth to hold back the pain
The night sweats
The voices that shout louder in my head
'You're tired'
'You're stressed'
So convinced with those words
'You are depressed'
That I became my biggest enemy
Angry
Lonely
Isolated
Deprived
Had become my sanctuary
Tired
Fat
Ugly
Not good enough
Were the words I repeated continuously
'I am not enough'
'I am a mess'
'I am the cause of so much stress
'I am exhausted'
'I am afraid'
'I am alone'
'I am lost'
'There's no one to come to my aid'

Soul of A Woman

'That's it'
'There is no cure'
Apart from the truth
The truth of who I Am
Just a body that's dead
A Mind that's empty
A soul that's given up
Standing at the edge of a bridge
Tears so warm yet so cold
'Can I really leave my story untold'
Broken hearts
Broken family
Broken Dreams
Or
Break the stigma
Speak up
And be BOLD

"Your Mind has the power to heal You or destroy You"

Life or Death is in the Power of the Tongue

I was speaking into existence and manifesting everything that I spoke. Words have power to heal you or destroy you and in this instance, I was destroying me. We often speak very negatively about ourselves and become what we speak about without realising. I was constantly repeating myself and how I felt: *'I'm not feeling well'*, *'I'm so exhausted'*, *'I'm tired'*, *'I'm depressed'*, *'I'm not myself'*. I didn't like listening to myself, and was creating the very life I didn't recognise or want.

Reflection

Words have power. They can transform a person's frown into a smile or smile into a frown. You have heard the saying *'Sticks and stones may break my bones, but words will never harm me'*. This is so untrue. Words can change your emotional state within seconds. So just imagine this: You are constantly insulting, putting down, bullying, and upsetting yourself with your words. Yet if someone does the same to you it will cause you to stop talking to them, even defending yourself. You may tell yourself time and time again that you don't care what they say to you. However if it comes from those you Love, then how would this affect you?

Why should it be any different with you? Why do we often choose to bully ourselves, yet not allow someone else to do the same?

There is a stigma around speaking up about mental health issues such as depression and anxiety. So we have a tendency to keep quiet. Thinking that we are protecting our Loved ones. However the more people open up about their own emotions the more people we heal as well as healing ourselves.

In this moment, when I was at the top of the bridge, I thought of my Loved ones that I would leave behind broken. Especially my beautiful daughter Jaida-Phoenix. In that moment of decision I decided not to inflict my pain on Her. I decided I had to reach out for help. I had a vision of my own funeral, the tears, the guilt, the anger my family would now carry as a result of my actions. I had to scream out loud just to be heard. I couldn't leave my story untold and neither should you.

YOU ARE THE MOST IMPORTANT PERSON ON THIS EARTH. **Without 'YOU' there would be no one that looked, behaved, smiled, talked, cried or acted like You. There would be this world without someone as unique and amazing as you.**

I Am Beautiful

I Am Strong

I Am Unique

I Am a Queen

I Am Kind

I Am a Diamond

I Am the creator of my life

Exercise 1

Affirmations are so powerful.

How about trying some for yourself?

Choose around 3 that really empower you and do the following:

Below write a minimum of 3, or more if you wish, affirmations starting with *I AM.....*

1.
2.
3.
4.
5.
6.
7.
8.
9.
10.

Exercise 2

Choose 3 - 5 of Your best ones that make you feel excited, make You smile and even if you don't believe them (yet) pick it just because if feels like an affirmation that you would Love to bring into your reality.

If You are unsure, here are some of my favourite ones.

They may be challenging to believe at first, however as You go through this journey, You will find ones that You do subconsciously that make You feel amazing daily.

My favourite ones are….

'I Am the creator of my life'
'I Am Amazing'
'I Am a Healer'
'I Am Strong'
'I Am a Poet'
'I Am a Queen'…. This is my daily mantra.
I also call every woman I meet a Queen as we are all Queens.

They Love it and trust Me You will too. It takes time and daily commitment to these affirmations.

*I Am.....*Stick your affirmations next to your bed, in your bathroom mirror and all the places as a reminder and when you see it, make sure You affirm it loud and smile.

I know this feels uncomfortable, but so does staying where You are.

"*Think like a Queen. A Queen is not afraid to fail. Failure is another stepping stone to Greatness.*"

Oprah Winfrey

Temptation

Like the forbidden fruit
We take that sinful bite
Suppressing our emotions
Knowing it's wrong whilst ignoring what is right
Our wants often mistaken for what our Soul truly desires
A touch
A kind word or that simple sentence *'It's going to be alright'*
We all seek Love
Connection
Importance
Instead we hate
Disconnect and simply accept our existence
'Just for this moment I want to feel good'
We listen to this voice and shut it down with *'Food alcohol drugs*
'Emotions You do not matter'
Our Mums always said *'Get it together'*
'How else Am I meant to feel better'
'I'm struggling to cope'
'Is there anyone or anything to give me Hope'
Guilt
Anger
Blame
'It's all too much...
'I'm the cause of all this shame'
'If only I could feel God's gentle touch'
'Your body is a temple' whispers our Creator *'It's the only one You have'*
So why fix it with a temporary artificial factor!!!
Temptation is life's challenge
Manifested by our fears that should not be ignored
Suppressed or cause us tears
It's a sign giving You a choice
'Do You give in and lose'
Or

Soul of A Woman

'Do You give in and face it'
Accept it
Embrace it and simply say loud and bold with so much
Confidence
'Temptation I see You…
Emotions I feel You…
Creator I hear You…
It really is my choice…
It's time for the world to hear my voice'

Happy Mother's Day

Upon my tireless breath
A life was born
Exhausted pain
Turned my shower of rain into a pleasurable gift
I gazed so lovingly at Your tiny little eyes
As You fought for my warmth
With Your frightened clammy little hands
I held You close so naturally
I had no idea what Love really felt like until You came from Me
and needed my Strength
The past was a distant memory
The doubt
The fear
The pain I endured
Just to have this meeting with You
This memory
This bond
I will do it again
Just to have the Love
That connects a Mother and child
You were born not just to be another number
You were born to heal Me
I Am not just a Woman
'I Am a Mother'

We Rise

We laugh together at times we argue

Always ending with a hug

You said *'You will always be my Mum I cannot hate You, our bond may be shakeable yet unbreakable'*

With a warm tear in this moment right here
I let go of the guilt of hurting You
When I wanted to end it all
I began to crawl
I had to do it my Angel
I had to learn to Love again
You saved Me my Angel
My Phoenix
We both Rise from the ashes
With Love together
We will never ever fall
It's never over until God says it's over

#motheranddaughtergoalz

Detox the Mind

I had spoken to so many people about how I felt. Some heard Me, offered advice, even tried to compare their current situation with mine, like it's a normal everyday thing. How could it be?

They couldn't possibly think that not sleeping due to having a new born baby to not sleeping because your mind is so negative the same feeling? So sometimes it was just so exhausting to explain what I was going through, so I'd shut down with: '*I Am ok*'. If only people knew that all I needed was to be HEARD, I mean really HEARD. Not have someone sympathise with Me, offer solutions, tell Me that I just needed to get back to work and smile?

I know they meant well, but this just caused Me to hide the ugly side of Me. Put my mask on and smile, shut down my feelings as after all '*Your feelings don't matter*' Right? Wrong. They are there for a reason and you will see why as you read on. Every time I returned home after a family party, a dinner with friends, the gym, a shopping trip, work that I hated, I came back more anxious, more exhausted, depleted and with a hand full of chocolates, a belly full of sugar and guilt written all over my face.

Reflection

We all have triggers, things that make us anxious It could be the past: pictures of your old self: watching people on Facebook, Instagram doing so well, looking so fit, especially those we used to hang around with; or simply trying to do normal everyday tasks like showering or cooking, but feeling too exhausted to do it: or even just seeing that cookie jar is enough to trigger us to unleash an emotion that either ranges from shame, guilt, frustration, anger, anxiety, fear and to some more extreme self-harm and suicidal thoughts.

Believe it or not, all the above were mine. I had to remove my triggers because they were slowly killing Me.

What are your triggers?

DID YOU KNOW THAT THE MIND NEEDS A DETOX BEFORE THE BODY CAN ACTUALLY SUSTAIN ONE IN ORDER TO CHANGE?

IN OTHER WORDS: YOU CANNOT CHANGE THE BODY UNLESS THE MIND IS RIGHT FIRST

Exercise 1

This one is going to be challenging, but challenges are what makes us grow.

List below your triggers, as many as you can think of.

1. My mum
2. My sister
3. My best friend
4. My kids
5. My job
6. My weight
7. My appearence
8. my finences
9. social media
10. Food

Now, Let's do a detox for the next 21 Days. The reason we focus on 21 is that it takes 21 days to develop a habit and we are focussing on removing the bad habits and replacing them with good healthy habits.

Remove yourself from all these triggers, the examples below are just some.

Social media

Delete all your apps: facebook, instagram, linkedin, snapchat, whatsapp groups, or even whatsapp completely so you don't find yourself going on them to check on others, or to get triggered by a message that you feel anxious about or obligated to answer. *Make a choice to call or text someone. This way no one can see if you have read a message and pressure you to answer. You do so on your terms.* *What you see on social media may not always be what is true. Everyone can hide behind a story, everyone is going through something we know very little about.*

Internet

This can be an obsession for the good and the bad. Switch your data off, no research, no analysing, no searching for answers. ' *All the answers are within you.*' Like a computer our brains can attract viruses and become frozen. Let's remove the virus and overload of information. *Analysis Paralysis* is real. Over Analyzing can cause you to *GET STUCK!!!*

Food

This one is tough if you have an issue around food, like I had. If I removed these foods from my house, I would go to the shop to buy them again, and if I had them at home when anxious or sad I would eat it all and feel guilty. So I say, keep them at home! Don't restrict yourself from anything. As you keep reading this book you will learn to listen to your emotions which will lessen the need to overeat, or, for some of you, undereat or not eat at all. When there is access to all things we don't feel the need to eat them or restrict them. For example when a child is told not to do/eat something, what do they do?

Going out

Although we need to be outdoors, sometimes we are so sensitive and emotional that being around others who are happy, in noisy places, in places that trigger us which leads to more shame, paranoia, depression and an increase of anxiety. Social Anxiety is real. So YES you must still live life, but in this case as we are starting in slow steps. Be selective as to whom you wish to spend your time with.

Ask yourself these questions to help you make a decision:

1. Does being around people energise me? Or deplete me? *Deplete me @ the moment*
2. Do I feel comfortable with a smaller group of people? *Yes*
3. Do I feel I can be myself around these people? *yes*
4. Do I feel they won't judge me? *yes*
5. Do I like being here?
6. When I return home, do I feel proud of myself for going?
7. Did it energise me? *yes*
8. Was it easy to make this decision? *NO*

Be wary of the doubts that will come, such as '*I feel tired*' '*I don't know what to wear*' '*What's the point on going out when I feel like crap when I'm there/return home*'? Focus on the positives and how you wish to live your life. Remember to challenge yourself as the negative voice will always *"try"* to win, but you have your own voice, listen to the *"winning"* voice. That's called your *"intuition"*.

If you answered yes to most of those questions, then do more of that. Surrounding yourself with positive people in positive vibes will uplift your mood.

So I'm a firm believer that when You remove something negative we must replace it with a positive so here is another exercise that balances out the one above...

Get Excited we are going back to our playfulness. Playing releases the imagination so let's play and connect with our *'Inner Child'*.

Exercise 2

 **Process of Removal and Replacing is Fun.**

The brain likes fun and imagination and freedom when it's filled with restriction. What do you now like to do that energises you and calms you resulting in smiling and breathing deep let's explore and like Nike says *'JUST DO IT'*. *When we Detox we focus on lots of Self-care rituals.* Here are a few.

CHECKLIST, TICK IT, DO IT! Focus on 3 a day... TIP: Just before bed open your calendar/diary and write down 3 things you enjoy doing and focus on at least doing 1 and ✓

Listen to Music

Calming music to calm you, Uplifting music to free you and release endorphins *(feel good hormone).*

Here are some song choices that helped me heal;

- India Arie *'I Am Light,* 'Beautiful' 'Worthy' 'Beautiful Flower' 'Strength Courage & Wisdom' 'Shoulda, Coulda, Woulda' 'I Am a Queen' 'Wings of Forgiveness, 'Breath' Beyonce *(The Lion King soundtrack),* Nina Simone *'I'm feeling good',*
- Ledisi, *'Forgiveness'*
- Hill St Soul, *'I smile'*
- Lia Renee Dior *'Good Morning'*
- Ciara *'I Love myself First' 'Level Up'* ☉
- Alicia Keys, *'Brand New Me'*

Dance like nobody's watching

No choreography here, just move. Self-expression sets you FREE and releases feel good hormones.

Listen to motivational videos

Lots on youtube. Motivational videos are FREE and instantly motivate you, my favourites are Oprah Winfrey, Iyanla Vanzant, Lisa Nichols, Les Brown, Will Smith, Steve Harvey, Tony Robbins, Wayne Dyer, Abraham Hicks, Law of attraction, Be inspired and many more. This rewires the brain to think positively.

Meditate upon waking for a minimum of 5-10mins

Lots on youtube. Focus on breathing deep. Lots of guided meditation videos you can do when you feel overwhelmed, anxious, tired and want to calm your mind.

My favourite is Deepak Choprah's 21 Days of Abundance meditation. You can start your own group to keep you motivated to keep it up. Remember it takes 21 Days to form a new habit.

Feel your Emotions

Be Still and allow yourself 5-10 mins to ask yourself why you are feeling anxious, angry, frustrated, tearful. And allow space to feel these emotions and let them be. Do a body scan whilst lying down and your body will tell you what it needs. DO NOT REACT instead BE STILL, BREATHE AND LISTEN TO YOUR EMOTIONS. Give them space to just release. They are asking to be heard and cared for. *#yourfeelingsmatter*

Eat 3 meals a day and 2 snacks a day

This allows your blood sugars to stabilize so you don't have high and low energy slumps that cause emotional eating, binge eating, drug abuse or alcohol excessive consumption.

Focus on eating every 3-4 hours, with time you will feel a rise of energy and emotional wellbeing. *'No more sugar cravings'.*

Allow yourself to Eat what you want

This is much more challenging when you have a not so good relationship with food. But the more you restrict the more you overeat that leads to guilt. Let go of the limitations. Likewise if you go hours without food and eat a biscuit or two. Remember energy for the Body is just as important as energy for the Mind so feed your Temple like you would a baby. '**YOU ARE YOUR ONLY LIMITATION'. Be like a child. You want it. Have it and Enjoy it. Guilty Free. If this seems too much of a struggle I can help you as this is my expertise. *'I GOT YOU'.***

Be in Nature

We are natural spiritual beings, needing fresh air, movement, water and food. When we breathe in air we feel free. So take a walk in the park and breathe. Go for a run if you have energy, exercise outdoors (lots of free bootcamps, fitness classes outdoors), simply get at least 30mins-1hr outside daily.

Move More

Yoga classes. These are natural, loving movements that reduce depression, anxiety by bringing calmness to your whole being and connects mind body and spirit through the power of breath. If you don't feel like joining a class *Youtube* has lots of videos on yoga for depression, anxiety, calm mind, sleep as well as many fitness classes. Everything to move your body. Focus on moving your body 30mins-1hr.

Outdoor fun - skipping is fun, playing ball, trampoline parks are all activities our inner child loves and you can do this with your loved ones or alone when you need an uplift. It works instantly.

If you are seeing a Doctor ask for *'Social Prescribing'*. This is a system where healthcare professionals are able to refer patients to local, non-clinical services to meet their wellbeing needs. What you can take part in will depend on what's available locally, and how local services work together. (examples are yoga classes, fitness classes, gym access, dance classes, arts classes, all free). As a Transformation coach and Wellbeing Holistic practitioner I am in partnership with my local council and provide my coaching programs that involve physical activity for people living within the Borough of Barking and Dagenham. If you are unable to go through your Doctor or he isn't able to help, contact your local Healthy living team and they will be able to assist you.

In some areas, a GP or nurse might refer you to a *'link worker'* – someone who meets with you to find out what you need, what you'd like to do, and then puts you in touch with a local organisation or group that can provide it. In other areas, the healthcare professional might put you directly in contact with a local group or organisation.

Remember not to get side tracked on researching for answers... K.I.S.S. ***KEEP IT SIMPLE STUPID!!!***

You are still detoxing, be gentle with yourself. Don't add in too much too soon.

This is just a few examples of some of the self-care rituals I do daily that have enabled me to heal and connect Mind and Body.

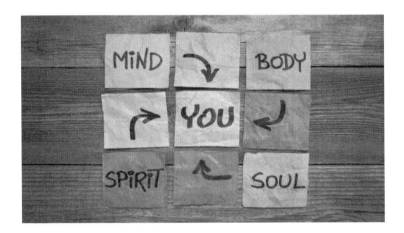

Exercise 3

Design your Daily and Evening Ritual

Something you do as soon as you wake up and before bed to calm and energise a very active Mind. Your Body will soon follow.

Focus on just 3 things upon waking and 3 things before bed. Below is a sample Ritual to help you format yours. Slowly make it part of your daily routine just like brushing your teeth.

Daily Ritual

6am - Wake up

3x I Am affirmations

Meditation - 10mins *(deep breathing)*

Motivational Video/Uplifting song – 5mins

3x things I am grateful for *we will cover this as we move forward in this journey

***THANK YOU I AM ALIVE...** is a good start*

LIKE A BABY WE HAVE TO LEARN WHEN TO SLEEP AND WHEN TO WAKE UP. REPEAT THIS DAILY AND SOON YOUR MIND WILL CONNECT WITH YOUR BODY IN ORDER TO GIVE YOU THE RESTFUL SLEEP YOU NEED.

Evening Ritual

10pm - Bedtime

3x things I Am grateful for *we will cover this as we move forward in this journey

Meditation for sleep – 5 mins

Finally let's do a *'Brain Dump'*

Write in your journal everything that is on your mind, '*let it out, breath it out, let it go'*.

Now *'Smile'* before you rest your head. Tomorrow is a brand new day.

YOU GET TO START OVER

NOW IT'S TIME TO DO YOURS....

My Daily Ritual

Time:............Wake up

I am grateful for....

1. Script letter
2. Affirmations
3. Audio / motivational video

....

(add more if you wish)

Brain dump

....

I love to....

Listen to Music

workout

Read

Meditate for 5-10mins – *deep breathing*

Listen to an inspiring song

Listen to a 5-10min motivational video – ***SET YOUR DAY RIGHT***

You can add more as you move through the journal when we get to the gratitude and self care list

---

Do this for 21 days. If you skip a day don't worry, continue on.

It takes 21 days to form a habit.

Fear

Born fearless
Into a world of the unknown
Free to explore wondrous gifts life has in store
As an innocent child
Born with one deep beautiful breath
A life I was given to adore
Born out of Love into Love
Where did that first red light of warning appear
Pumping blood into my tiny little veins
Causing my tiny little organs to freeze
As though a hunter lay hidden to destroy Me and keep Me still
Was it my Mother's painful heart
That caused Her voice to sound like a lionesses' roar
When I almost fell out of my cot
Or my Fathers' angry roar
Like a Lion hunting for His prey
The bass of his voice deafening my tiny little ears with an
unfamiliar
'DO NOT TOUCH' followed by a sting to the back of my tiny
little soft hand
Causing Me to flinch, close my eyes, and feel my heartbeat
And cry of pain to feel my Mother's warm embrace
To hear Her nurturing voice whispering softly
'It's ok baby You mustn't touch that'
Does this thing that causes so much distress in a person's life
I know I'm not the only one frozen in despair
Because of this thing I cannot see or touch
Yet I can feel it
So suddenly upon waking
It appears in such a rush
Is it simply that it does not really exist
This terrifying force I allow to persist
That causes so much tension
So much pain
Blood pumping panic strikes my veins

Soul of A Woman

'STOP'
'BREATHE'
Eyes wide shut
Inhale 1 2 3 4 5
Hold 6 7 8
Exhale 9 8 7 6 5 4 3 2 1
Inhale 1 2 3 4 5
Hold 6 7 8
Exhale 9 8 7 6 5 4 3 2 1
'It's reducing'
The heart pumping sound is slowing down
Inhale 1 2 3 4 5
Hold 6 7 8
Exhale 9 8 7 6 5 4 3 2 1
'I'm ok'
'I'm Alive'
There is no danger
'I will survive'
'WAIT'
I cannot feel it anymore
My breath bought calmness
Peace in just a few seconds
Yet nothing happened
Let Me question what just occurred
'What caused this feeling to emerge'
'A thought of what could happen'
'An image of tomorrow'
'A worry of my future'
'What could happen'
'Yet nothing happened'
'It hasn't happened yet'
'Will it actually happen'
'I simply thought of it'
Causing my hands to sweat
My blood to rise
Making Me suffocate
Bringing in endless thoughts
Out of control yet out of Mind

Soul of A Woman

'In my Mind'
'Yes in my Mind'
Hold up
'Wait a minute'
Rewind
'In my beautiful Mind I created the feeling through a thought
or image'
'Then I made it disappear'
'How Do I do it'
Rewind right back
It was something in my power I do not lack
The Breath
'I focussed on it'
'Listened to it'
My organs became still
Calm
Peaceful
'YES that's all I did'
'That's all I did'
A smile spreads across my face
I became *'Present'*
Still in my thoughts
Maybe next time I can try and bring an image
Something I really want
Nature
Waterfalls
Butterflies
Warm chocolate covered marshmallow dripping in my tongue
'Yummm'
'I can create my own Future'
'Be in control of my destination using my own beautiful Mind'
'I can give myself the gift'
'A Present I can have at anytime'
'This feeling of uncertainty'
'This feeling of an internal fight'
'This feeling I deeply hated causing me to freeze'
'To almost destroying Me'
'Controlling my life'

Soul of A Woman

Let Me be forever Grateful for this feeling I now call my
"Friend"
Who came into my life so uninvited
So unexpected
Stimulated
Unprotected
Yet it came for a reason and will often come in seasons
To guide Me
To protect Me
To move Me
To excite Me
To challenge Me
To grow Me
To elevate Me
To teach Me a lesson
'Thank You Fear for being there to the end'
'Thank You Fear for being my Bestest Friend'

Anxiety

Don't be afraid of what You see
When You see Your reflection in Me
Don't think You should do more or be perfect
To be the best that You can be

Look into my eyes full of excitement
Even if there's fear
You may not like what You hear
Yet my words will set You Free
They did for Me
So why won't You allow my words to penetrate into Your Soul
Listen to my voice
Read about my journey
Connect through my poetry
I am a woman with scars
I don't claim to be perfect not by far
I was a giver
I gave my all
With no expectations
Whilst You stood tall
My vulnerability mistaken for weakness
You finally had Me at my weakest
You thought I remained there
That You could take back control of my emotions
Until I discovered my vulnerability was my awakening
Hmmmm the Freedom I felt when I realised *'I Am a Woman of Worth'*
A Woman of Power
A Goddess so sexy and strong
A Queen of my Kingdom
Worthy of a King
Confidence oozed from every curve that I sensuously hold
My body Beautifully carved by my Creator
Greatly appreciated by my King
A voice so real and engaging

Soul of A Woman

That cuts so deep like a knife
So it's better for You to push Me away
My truth are like daggers the size of an elephant with a roar of
a Lioness that You cannot hide from
Wait did I not say *'Do not be afraid of the reflection You see*
when You look directly at Me'
Yet don't be jealous of Me
You are worthy of a life that seems so impossible yet is waiting
for You to say
'I Am Worthy'
Let Me guide You to see the Power and Unique Diamond that
resides in You
I Am not better than You
I Am better than yesterday's Me
I Am not perfect nor do I ever wish to be
Perfection is a perception
Don't ever desire to be perfect
Desire to be Free
Let me tell You a secret so shocking
So Powerful
So Transformational that once I tell You
It won't remain a secret
Instead it will open the door which desires the key
The secret is...
You are already Free
Because You hold the key to healing the pain by accepting that
You are
An *'Imperfectly Perfect Reflection of Me'*
A Woman
Take a deep breath
Get comfortable being uncomfortable
Just believe that the Power is within
Anxiety You are my Saviour
I Am ready to Begin

Journey of Acceptance

The first step towards change was *'Self-acceptance'*. I hated where I was, who I had become and everything about me. I was desperate for change. I often heard many people, especially Christians saying that I must *'surrender'* and *'give thanks'*. How could I when I was lost and carried this feeling of lack, fear, extreme fatigue, one I could not explain. I barely slept, I couldn't even smile, my laughter felt forced, fake. I felt like I was 'dead inside'. So how could I possibly accept and give thanks?

Reflection

Acceptance meant accepting where I was and that I got myself here. If I wanted change I had to do things I enjoyed doing when I was well or doing things that I wanted to do but felt anxious to do so.

Not listening to the voices that kept saying *'you are too tired, you are depressed, people will see you are not well'* But the voices came with an AFFIRMATION OF *'I AM TIRED, I AM DEPRESSED, I LOOK SICK, I LOOK DISGUSTING!'* All of these negative affirmations affirmed what I felt and believed. They kept me stuck. I became the words I was very familiar with. I became, anxious, depressed, sick, tired, exhausted, ugly, never get better, terrible Mother, insomniac. Someone I didn't like or recognise.

I had to challenge myself to accept all invitations from all friends/family I trusted and felt comfortable and most importantly that didn't judge me or tell me what to do. They gave me the space to be as I was, they accepted me.

Exercise 1

Answer below, put down the first answer that comes to your mind, these are the most honest, it's your subconscious mind speaking back at you, listen and write it down...now go!!!!

What are you afraid of but want to do it?

_Leave my Job, Go outside
with my kids. See people I know
Build my social media platform_

If there was no feeling of fear/depression/worry/blame/guilt, what would you be doing right now?

_Working on my blog, Qualify as a life +
wellness coach, workout daily. Go out
with my kids, Post on social media_

What did the old you before the problem, whatever that may be, usually do?

_Workout, Take my kids out,
Post on social media, Meet with
friends. Went on dating Apps.

Drive whenever I wanted_

What is the worst thing that can happen if you do it?

Peoples opinions, Judgement

How will you feel when this happens?

Anxious

What is the best thing that can happen if you do it?

Life will Start Improving, I Will be happier. Finance will Improve. I will be enjoying extra Things

How will you feel when this happens?

HAPPY, excited, Motivated to do More. enjoying things, Free, Calm

How do you want to feel?

Free, HAPPY, excited, Hopeful

Centering Exercise

Take 5 Deep breaths in through your nose and out through your mouth and repeat *'I AM CALM, I AM PRESENT, I ACCEPT MYSELF, I AM RELAXED.'*

GET A NEW JOURNAL. Make sure it's pretty and you will use it to journal EVERYTHING you feel about Yourself and do the following...

Exercise 2

 Write a letter of acceptance

I Accept ...

This is your first exercise and the one that will begin the catalyst to change. Remember slow steps. Make sure you are calm, alone and ready to take the First Step.

Write down all the things that have happened to you leading to where you are. Some painful memories may stir emotions that you haven't allowed in for a while, release your tears, anger and don't suppress this emotion. It's a must for this exercise to work. Go deep (i.e *I accept that I allowed myself to fall so deep in...I accept that some people/circumstances have...*

End this letter with *'I Am now willing to accept that I am responsible for where I Am in my life and I commit to moving forward and doing whatever it takes to feel ...*

Sign it with your name and date. Now Thank yourself for doing this. I know it wasn't easy!

 Write a list of things you are grateful for...

'I Am grateful for ....

No matter how small. It could be *'I Am grateful for the water, the sun, my children, or simply because I am grateful to be alive'*. I know you may not feel grateful, but gratitude leads to more things to be grateful about. Begin with this statement for every line. *'I Am grateful for...'*

A good exercise is to do this before retiring for bed and upon waking just a simple self-talk *'I Am grateful for today'*.

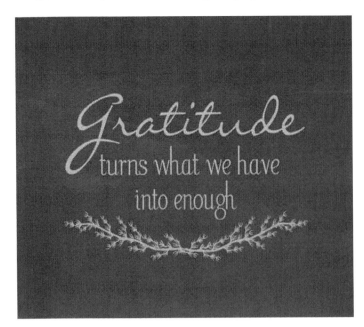

Acceptance is
Key to truly
be free

Free2embraceme

"Our deepest fear is not that we are inadequate. Our deepest fear is that we are Powerful Beyond Measure"

Nelson Mandela

Fearless

That feeling intensifies bringing my hot brown soft skin so
alive
Tiny goosebumps pouring from my pores
Breathlessly breathing trapped mindlessly confused
overwhelmed
Scream louder *'I can't do it'*
'What if I mess up'
'I don't know enough'
'I Am not good enough'
'I Am not enough'
Uncomfortably comfortable stay where You are kind of safety
that's unsafe yet protected
Now breathe
Scream or just say *'I'm not ready'*
Only to feel that sense of importance or appreciation
Or even empowerment slip away from Your fingers back to
that hamster wheel Groundhog Day vicious cycle of
suffocation that whispers
'Better the devil You know'
Rather than stretch Yourself and grow
If You grow the whole world would know
The Power of Your Strength and feel somewhat weaker
Inferior in Your presence
Think that You have it all together
Leave You be and not help You
This fear of growth engulfs You
Keeps You locked in Your Beautiful Mind
Locking a *'Diamond'* so unique
Yet so Divine
Till one day You make a choice
To stop caring what others think
To Live life Your way
To leave Your past where it should stay
Head up high
Eyes wide shut

Soul of A Woman

Gratitude is Your greatest Altitude
Your voice stops shaking
Your Fear becomes Your "making"
No longer quiet nor speechless
You speak out loud
'I Am FEARLESS'

"She had to breakdown before She could crawl, die to self and spread Her wings, learn to be grateful for the smallest of things"

The Gifted

Mindfully calm
Intellectually sharp
Neurolinguistics visualising Dreams
Overstimulating thoughts
Visions of Greatness
Engaging simultaneously
Realms so vibrant
Mentally enticing senses
Aspiring choices
Thoughts becoming things thus actionable
Entering into a world of Your internal reality of who You are
Inspiring others through Your pain
Accepting Your Present
Motivating others through Your Essence
Your Presence
Embracing all the beauty that lies within
Realising our Creator is in control
Empowering others to have Faith
Freedom to be who You desire to be
Trusting in Your Power
Your God given Strength
Overcoming challenges
Letting go
Owning up to Your full potential
Visualising the future
Embracing the present
Loving and claiming Your Gift
You are Gifted beyond measure

"Inspiration is the Greatest Gift it opens the door to many Possibilities"

Searching

In search of freedom You'll never find

In search of happiness to fulfil You inside
In search of better health to feel better now
In search of a quick fix
STOP right there
REWIND
'What is wrong with You' Your inner voice shouts
Look around
How many times do You look externally
Comparing Yourself to someone You physically admire
Jealously wishing You looked like them
Yet know nothing about who they are
What they do
What they hide behind the mask
The Perfect body
Fake smile
Or even fake words
Look within
Not without
Your eyes perceive what You lack
START looking forward
STOP going back
Begin to ask Yourself
'How can I be FREE'
'What brings Me Happiness'
'What do I need to focus on to feel better'
'What small steps can I take to get me from here to there'
Then begin where You are
Thank Yourself for getting this far
Discover who You are
Be still and hear Your Higher voice
Your Higher Spirit
The Goddess within
Speak into Existence

Soul of A Woman

Be Grateful for Your Persistence
Be silent
Hear the voice of Your subconscious
It has Power to Inspire You
Or destroy You
You are the Creator of Your life
The Conductor of Your destiny
God gave You a Spirit of a sound mind
The voice to speak out Loud
The body with incredible abilities
'As You thinketh so shall You become'
You have the power to connect with Your inner Goddess
And become One
What You seek
You already have
What You act upon
You already are
What You speak
You have become
The search is already here
Mindfully
Visualise
Your life and how You have arrived at this destination
Isn't by coincidence
Or accident
Or anyone's fault but Your own
End the struggle
Cut the blame
Say *'Hello'* to the life You desire
Choose through Your words
You have the Power to end the pain

"You hold the key to healing the pain by accepting that You are an imperfectly perfect reflection of Me"

Journey of Letting Go

The second step was to *'Let Go'*. I was so stuck in the past, wishing to return to the old me. Believing that if I could go back and be myself again then I would be better and live life happily again. I was so wrong.

The past is in the past, I can't change it or go back to it. It came to teach me many lessons. It came to bring me a *"Present"* a *"Gift"* which I continuously keep, secretly. Up until this *"Present"* moment I was merely surviving on my own. I repeat *"on my own"* believing that I had to do it *'All alone'* yet there was a Greater force within me that had the belief but wasn't actually asking for the "Guidance". I needed to strengthen that belief.

"Faith the size of a mustard seed can move mountains"

Matthew 17:20.

I had the seed it just needed nurturing to grow. So I asked for my faith to grow.

Reflection

To Let go meant I had to surrender. So I did. I made a decision that I could no longer keep going back to the past in my mind. It was full of guilt, *'shoulda, coulda, woulda'* that I have no control over anymore, full of shame that I shouldn't feel, lots of self-blame, even blame on others and so painful it was a trigger. I had to be *'Present'* to *'Embrace'* my *'Gift'*. I realised that I was carrying so much baggage that my neck and my shoulders actually physically felt heavy.

I remember years ago when I left my relationship with my daughter's Father that I was in extreme agony before I made the decision that I was no longer happy. The guilt that I carried of breaking up our family when my daughter was only 2 years old was so much that I had to seek professional medical support. I had steroids, acupuncture, medication and nothing worked. Until I was finally true to myself and released Him. As I let Him go a weight I carried also left.

I simply surrendered to what I no longer had control over and released the weight, I was *"FREE"* to be Me. And guess what

Me is *"Liberating"*, can you feel the smile on my face as you say those words and smile too?

At times we find it so hard to *'Let go'*. I struggled with this especially when I was in church and they kept on going on about *'letting go'*. It frustrated me as I had no idea what that meant. I wasn't using my faith the church assistants would say. Yet no one could help me to 'let go'. I even went as far as Baptism, three times, once in my home in my own bath then in churches twice. Every time I came out of it I felt exactly the same. I was desperate for the miracle to happen as they said it would. I felt like a failure. So I stopped trusting in churches, having had my own experiences of trusting those who say they are from the Lord, yet seeing that their words never actually reflected their actions.

I pulled away from seeking a *'God'* outside of myself and I searched within. Guess what? I found out He was always within me. Yet my conversations with Him had to start and they did.

Action

Now it's time for you to *'Let Go'* too. There is no ritual, no magic tricks, no gimmicks to this. It simply is removing the bag off your shoulders and *'aaaahhhh'*.

Exercise 1

 **LET'S WRITE ANOTHER LETTER.**

want you to do the centering exercise. Focus on a
. As this will release emotions you are oppressing
your love and attention, so calmness is key.

Centering Exercise

Take 5 Deep breaths through your nose and out your mouth
and repeat *'I AM CALM, I AM PRESENT, I ACCEPT MYSELF, I
AM NOW WILLING TO LET GO, I AM LETTING GO....*

Get a blank piece of A4 paper, not your journal. Begin to write
all the things you are holding onto that no longer serve you,
that trigger you, deplete you, upset you, anger you and
frustrate you. People, circumstances, jobs, ex partners, things
people said, even loved ones, blame, shame, guilt, failure,
pain, bring them all up.

This exercise is very important. What we often constantly
bombard our minds with is negative past thoughts. We inherit
our own perception of what someone is like towards us and
turn it into a negative when we are in a negative state of
mind. It's time to *'Release it all.'*

Exercise 2

Take that same piece of paper whilst you are going through
the emotions. Here is the fun part. Be safe though. Either
outside or on your kitchen sink with running water.

Get a lighter out and burn that sucker out.

Let it dissipate whilst you repeat the centering exercise...'*I LET GO, I RELEASE, I AM FREE'*.

Heart Exercise

Take a moment after you have finished. Allow your emotions to be, don't suppress instead be "*STILL*" and really feel them. Place your hand on your heart and repeat the Centering Exercise. Then ask yourself *'What do I need right now'* and listen. Your body will talk back to you.

Now you must celebrate it. Put on your favourite upbeat song of empowerment. Dance like nobody's watching , inhale Love, exhale Freedom.

Connect with your inner child, *'You are FREE'*.

What does it mean to surrender?

The act of stopping fighting and officially admitting defeat:

I could no longer control what I was holding onto. I realised I could not do this on my own. I was tired of fighting, tired of hurting, tired of the pain. Someone else had to help me. I had to release this burden and weight on my shoulders. A simple letter was the start, the action I had to take. But the feeling that came with the words I spoke out loud in my own bedroom was my own surrendering.

Once you release surrendering comes.

'God I no longer care what is going on with me, please Bless me so I can Bless others'

This was by far my most powerful prayer. Realising there was something bigger than me that was going to carry me, a *"Higher Power"* I had never connected with. This prayer started a chain of actions that followed many conversations with God.

I surrendered in this very moment. *'Free2Embrace Me'* was born from this prayer.

Once again my Creator answered my prayers.

Life's Journey

No Road is ever straight
No path is ever narrow
Life is like a box of chocolates
There are no guarantees of tomorrow
Anxiously screaming for answers
'What are these butterflies dancing in my stomach'
Feels like a bag drowning my breath
Like a light switch has gone off
Deep in darkness I lay lost
Yet afraid to open them
Cursing the sun for its shining warmth
Hating the birds for their joyful sounds
In bed I lay lifeless
Reciting negativity to this body I hate
Disconnecting mentally to this world
Disconnecting physically a story yet untold
The bigger the challenge
The harder the fall
I am here for a purpose
No matter what I will stand tall

"A woman in harmony with Her spirit is like a river flowing. She goes where She will without pretence and arrives at Her destination prepared to be Herself and only Herself."

Maya Angelou

A Diamond is Born

Playful sounds dancing mindlessly
As nature calls upon my first Breath
The calm before the storm
The light before the darkness
Surrounded by water before the dryness
Ripped away from a comfort so warm and safe
A place so familiar
So Peaceful
Where voices are distant and reassuring
Often loud and even disturbing
Yet safe and sound
Where colourful bubbles are found
Floating in a blissful cloud
Discovering through darkness
Growth
Restricted daily
Weekly
Monthly
Pushing away external movement and touches
Laying in an internal world where no judgement or fear exists
Nor pain or even shame persists
Innocently Freely moving
Developing Naturally
'WAIT' I plead
Something externally breaks that cycle of comfort
Bringing light with so much noise
Objects and weird strangers in masks
Hearing cries from a woman's pain
'Breathe Breathe Breathe'
A voice with so much strain yet familiar and loving
'PUSH' a familiar voice roars
Pulling forcefully my tiny head
'No it's not that time, I'm not Ready yet'
To be ripped by this force
Bringing emotions I cannot express

Soul of A Woman

'It can't be that time yet' I cry
To face an unfamiliar realm or dimension I wasn't prepared for
OK Breathe
'No...Scream...
...YES cry'
No sound
My lungs are so tight that I scream so loud
Yet no one can hear me
'I'm suffocating'
'Why is no one listening' I stutter
Grabbing
Shacking
Smack smack smack
'OUCH that's painful'
Scream loud
Cry louder
'IT'S A GIRL'
My nurturer's arms holding me tightly to Her chest
I feel safe again
Comforted
Warm
I Exhale 'arhhhh'
A calming presence fulfils this bondness we share
Our Hearts beat a rhythm so sweet
I open my tiny eyes slowly
She opens Her eyes full of tears
This pain She suffered
The challenges She faced
The hurt they caused Her
The shame She felt
The abuse She took
The loneliness She felt
Through what She thought was Love
In this moment
She exhaled *'arhhh...'*
Staring into my tiny little brown eyes and whispered through
Her joyful heart
'Hello my Angel'

Soul of A Woman

'My sweet little girl'
'I will shower You with Love'
'Dress You in Diamonds...
And cover You with Pearls'

"Beauty cannot be seen or touched. Beauty is felt with the heart"

Ready to Shine

Tears are a symbol of pain
Joy
Contentment
Freedom and Victory
A reminder that Strength and Love Live within me
No challenge too big
No mountain too high
No valley too low
No river too deep
This journey has been so bitter sweet
Life as I Lived it taught Me many lessons
People I met
Trusted
Supported and gave my all
Often than not misunderstood Me
Abused Me
Confused Me
Took from Me
Refused to Accept Me
Yet their perceptions and judgements contributed to Me
Almost destroying Me
I was strong to their eyes
Behind the smile lay many white lies
'I am fine'
'I'm independent'
'I got's Mine'
Falling deeper in debt of lack of Love for Myself
Helping others with Love
Giving unconditionally in small gestures
Covered with hearts
Delivered with doves
What I had I simply gave
Emptying my bank
To deposit into those who needed
Wanted

Soul of A Woman

Knew I would give
Yet never returned
That girl died in December 2017
Only to Rise like a Phoenix filled with Love
Strength
And Resilience
I woke up to my Dream
The Purpose God created within
A reason to Live gave birth to a Limitless Creative
Loving
Passionate Spiritual Being
My only lesson from High Above is to spread Love
To pass on my teachings
So no one else that comes to Me will ever suffer endlessly
To give them Hope of the Present
To ignite tomorrow's mystery
To let go of the past that they needed
And step into a world they can Create
Through their Mind's eye
To Embrace the Spirit that lies within
To finally say *'I Am Alive'*
'I Am a Diamond'
'I Am Ready to Shine'

Ready to say *'YES'*

Her vision so clear
That even a blind man can see
Her Strength is Her weakness
Driven by Her Vulnerability
So clear is the sky that birds freely fly
Many disruptions erupt Her mind
Yet Her vision is so Alive
Do not fear Her presence
Do not mute Her voice
Do not sit in awe
Wondering about Her Allure
Instead tread Her steps
Let Her guidance endure
The door is here
The key You so securely hold
Unlock it don't be afraid
Her guidance is Your aid
Don't stop this flow of words cause I write with my Mind
The words simply flow from my inner guide with pride
Tears flow in floods
As I speak out louder
I heal as You heal cause together we are so much Stronger
Your retreat to Self-love is a start of Your journey
It's ready for You to walk through with Your key
Let down Your pride
Your lack or doubt
See Your value when You say
'YES I AM READY'

Journey of Forgiveness

The third Step is by far the hardest, most challenging, yet a step we all must take. A path of forgiveness to ourselves, for where we are. Once I learned to forgive myself, I was able to be grateful for everything that I had done, didn't do, had and now have, no matter how little.

I never knew I needed to forgive myself in order to forgive others, because I didn't blame anyone else, I thought. But as I went into this journey of forgiving myself, I was able to identify where I was subconsciously blaming others for my lack, and once I was able to forgive myself, I uncovered where I also needed to forgive others.

Reflection

The lesson I learned here is that I was the only one to blame for my current situation because I allowed myself to get to this *'Present Moment'* which meant I had choices and chose this very same life I was living. So I had to forgive myself first.

What did I need to forgive myself for?

I had become so fixated with my body, and fixing it. When I began my fitness journey as a Personal Trainer, helping women to transform their bodies, I had no idea how the advice I gave them about what they should and shouldn't eat came with no balance. In my mind, I thought as an *"Action"* person did. You want something done: neglect your feelings and your thoughts and just *'DO IT'*. As I got more in tune with my female clients, the more I realised that the search for the *'PERFECT BODY'*, or even *'INCREASING CONFIDENCE'*, all came from a physical place that was actually messing up their Mental and Emotional wellbeing.

I have always reflected my clients and they reflect me. So If I'm looking, acting, being a certain way I will be drawn to them. I lead by example. My muscles, my restrictions, even carrying my containers of food according to my *'Bodybuilders diet',* all contributed to this search for the *'PERFECT BODY'.* I wasn't accepting this beautiful body I have, *"my temple".* Instead I was always trying to change it with the next magic *'diet'* and passing this onto my clients.

I realised after years of suffering, that my Mental and Emotional wellbeing was actually more important than the physical, because the physical was only reflecting what was on my mind.

Remember that *'Affirmations'* are Powerful? They were. Listen to what my mind was telling me...

'I am tired' 'I don't like my muscles, they are looking too big' 'I don't care what they say about me looking too muscular, it's what I have to do to look perfect' 'I Am exhausted' 'I can't eat these things, I will get fat', 'I feel so drained' 'I don't feel or look like me anymore'. The list became worse as I was labelled *'DEPRESSED'.* You know what a bully does and says? I was my worst bully.

I had to forgive myself for mistreating my mind and my body, and suppressing my emotions for 4.5 years. It was very difficult and uncomfortable, silly at times, extremely emotional; however I still look back at my pictures, my poems and I cry tears of joy. I tell myself constantly *'I Am glad I never competed as a Fitness Model'.* This was again God's message.

Picture on left size 8 body building days July 2013. I trained 6 days a week and followed a very strict bodybuilders diet. Picture on right November 2019 size 10. No diets, no strict training regimes, no rules.

Exercise 1

 **I love writing letters.**

When we express ourselves with pen and paper, our emotions flow so much easier than when we speak. It also eases the mind because you are focussing on your thoughts and extracting them out of your overwhelmed, exhausted mind; then putting it visually where you can see what you are holding onto. So, you see how we have to continue to let go of the weight we choose to carry? We are always the conductors of our lives and the destiny that we decide. There is no such thing as fate. However, there is this purpose we are born with: yet only some listen to its voices and command it. As genie says *'Your wish is my command'* isn't entirely true, however *'Your wish is your command'* so go *'Do the work'*.

Get your beautiful Journal out. This one's for keeps. It's a love letter from you to you.

Centering Exercise

Take 5 Deep breaths through your nose and out your mouth and repeat *'I AM CALM, I AM PRESENT, I ACCEPT MYSELF, I LET GO, I AM WILLING TO FORGIVE MYSELF, I FORGIVE MYSELF...*

Write a letter Forgiving yourself for everything, no matter how big or small.

Date it...

Dear [your name]

'I forgive You for.......' In this one you are in control, forgiveness is your own journal entry. **HINT**: Remember to forgive your parents too. Our parents do what they can with that they know. They too need forgiveness, not for them but for you.

Exercise 2

We haven't finished yet. I want you to end the letter with**...**

'I Am now willing to learn to trust You'. Sign it with your name and seal it with an envelope and plant it with a kiss.

Heart Exercise

Take a moment after you have finished. Allow your emotions to be, don't suppress instead be *"STILL"* and really feel them. Place your hand on your heart and repeat the *Centering Exercise*. Then ask yourself *'What do I need right now'* and listen. Your body will talk back to you. You're one step closer to trusting you.

Any relationship takes time and patience. Be patient your healing is happening subconsciously and soon consciously it will shine through.

See page 125 for Self-care ideas you can now do for yourself. Because after forgiveness embracing you and trusting in your body begins ...*Are you ready beautiful?*

"*To Inspire another who is uninspired is like living Your purpose. Inspire one Inspire All*"

Your Embrace

Isolated mindlessly
In a world created by Her Mind
Overwhelming thoughtlessly
In so much sorrow
So much anger
So much pain
Negatively uttering words continuously
'I don't feel myself' She cries
'You will never get the best of Me' She screams
Eyes so lost
A heart full of pain
Brokenness yet desperate to Heal
Denying Herself what She truly Desires
All so She can please another
So much guilt
She cried out to You
God yelled loudly *'Go answer'*
'Be Her Friend'
'Her Guide'
'But deny Your Desires of the flesh'
'No intentions'
'No expectations'
'Heal Her pain'
'Let Her pain Heal Yours'
'Be Her Saviour when She calls'
'Deny Your feelings'
'Hide who You truly are'
'Be Her Armour'
'Her Light'
'Win Her Trust'
'Do not confuse Love for lust'
Again She cried out for You
You Held Her close and whispered softly
'We've never kissed'

Soul of A Woman

She leaned close to Feel Your lips
Forgetting Her pain with just one kiss
Time stopped
So tenderly You Felt Her soft brown skin
With just one touch You melted *'Her Heart'*
Freedom overcame Her
Mindlessly She opened up
Trusted
Let Go
Forgetting everything yet lost in each other's Soul
Your bodies connected
Like yin and yang
Unashamedly
You both opened *'Your Hearts'*
Fearlessly
Her inner Sexiness
Her Devine Goddess
Desired eagerly
Connected Sensuously
That night You took Her pain away
That night You both finally
Exhaled

Passion flows through You to Me

Those Hazel gazing eyes
See through my Soul with no lies
Your presence in my world came as an uninvited Surprise
So Warm
So Gifted
So Calm
So Kind
No judgement
No expectations
No price
You pulled Me close with Your strong Embrace
I heard Your Heart scream loud
Whispering
'I Feel Your pain'
'You will learn to Dance in the rain'
So intellectually we Connected in a world we called our Own
You in Your thoughts
Me in mine
Neither of us thought that our Journey would be so Divine
You picked up my burdens
One by one You took them away
Anger I brought Love into Your Life
Guilt You told Me it's not mine to keep
Blame You showed that my Vulnerability was my biggest
Strength
That night You opened up
Our guilty Pleasures became our most Passionate Treasures
Without caressing Me
I felt Your Passion
Your hungry intentional eyes devoured Me
Sensed Me
Wanted Me
Without barriers my lips touched Yours
So Passionately You pulled Me close
I sensed You
Needed You

Soul of A Woman

Without shame
You undressed Me
Caressed Me made Me Feel Alive
Burning Desire through My blood filled veins penetrated into
Your aaahhhh
[DEEP BREATH]
You Guided Me with Your deep voice working mentally in my
wondrous Mind
Pulling Me down into Your world
Your touch
Your deep demanding voice *'Lay Down'*
Obeying like a Child ready for *"Her treat"*

Hearing Passionate whispers
Burning deep within my femininity
Eyes closed to a feeling *'soooo hmmmm'*
[DEEP SATISFYING BREATH]
Connecting Engaging so Passionately
Brown skin to brown skin our bodies rhythmically Dancing so
Sweet
So Alive
So Sexy
So Empowering
So in too deep
We Connect our Love unconditionally

Self-Love

Stripped naked I stand
Head low
Shoulders slumped forward
Avoiding eye contact
Vulnerable
Ashamed
Her reflection stares back at Me
His deep voice asks Lovingly
'What do You see'
Silently I whisper to myself
'I don't see what You see'
Holding Me He whispers
'Look at You, You're Beautiful'
He challenges Me to look again
My reflection talks back to Me
'He is right but only You can see the Beauty that is within You
is Yours to set You FREE'
'Look at Me She whispers, it's ok'
Too afraid to listen
Too disgusted to look
'It's ok You are safe' She whispers
Reassuring me that it's just Her and Me
[DEEP BREATH]
'What Am I afraid of'
She shouts louder with Faith *'You can do it, I Am Your Spirit I'll*
set You FREE'
Head up
Shoulders back
I ask Myself *'What do I see'*
I see pain
I see fear
'I don't see Me'
'You are Beautiful' He proudly says with conviction
I let go of the fear
The touch of His hand awakens Me

Soul of A Woman

I begin with my curly kinky hair compelled in a hot mess from
the night before
'I Love You I whisper'
His Hazel eyes gazing silently
My deep dark brown eyes full of pain blinded by tears
'I Love You'
My soft big lips that show that *'I am an African Queen'*
'I really Love You'
A smile full of Love brightens my face
He smiles admiring Me
My full tiny pert breasts *'I really love You'*
You have nurtured my Own and are always getting me into
trouble
He winks playfully squeezing ever so sensuously
A small laugh escapes my mouth
A naughty smile caresses my femininity
My stomach
Hmm a little bloated from the neglect and emotional
suppression
'I still love You regardless, YES I love You stomach'
*'You have carried my Creation for 9 months and You still look
amazing'* I whisper to myself
'YES I do Love You'
My hips and big black ass
*'Oh Yasssss I Love and thank You for how You make tight
dresses fit so Perfectly'*
His greedy eyes answer sexually
Hmm a tingle excites Me
My thighs
*'I truly most definitely Love You for Your Strength and Your
shape arrrhhhhh'*
I start back from the top
'Do You dare me to stop'
*'I Am **N**atural'*
*'I Am **E**mpowered'*
*'I Am **U**nique'*
*'I Am **S**exy'*
*'I Am **A**mazing'*

Soul of A Woman

*'I Am **C**ourageous'*
*'I Am **A**uthentic'*
*'I Am **T**rusting'*
*'I Am **O**mnificent'*
*'I Am **J**oyful'*
*'I Am **A**bundant'*
'I Am the Beauty that I perceive Me to be'
His thoughts mirror mine
'YES I AM HIS AFRICAN QUEEN'
Beauty is not how I look
What clothes I wear
What makeup I use
'Beauty is the Goddess that Lives within Me'

This picture was captured by my King, Simon Robinson in November 2017

They say that behind every successful man there is a greater woman. I had lost all self-belief and hated my body. I had no idea where to begin, He guided me.

I was inspired to use this picture as my cover. As it was this very moment that I asked myself 'How can I Love Me?'
The mirror was my own self-reflection that I began to talk to and still do daily, naked and vulnerable.

Exactly what nature intended for Me. I Am no longer ashamed of my Body.

I Love every part of Me.

So Beautifully Carved

Pure heart of an innocent Soul
Vulnerable
Beautiful
Covered in Gold
Graciously sculptured with intricate lines
Carefully Created by the finest hands
With an eye detail so visually defined
Every inch
Every curve designed to feel so Divine
Eyes so soft with a deep gazing stare
So striking
So focussed
That even a blinded Soul would feel naked
A nose so distinctive not to be teased but embraced
The lines of Her African lips
Pencil defined so carefully drawn that the touch of Her own
finger would bring a sense so unknown
The softness of Her mouth
As Her tongue gently moistens Her pout
Her jaw confidently raised to reveal Her neck that's so open to
Her vocally
Speaking words of Power and Strength that She holds deep
within
The rise of Her chest that uplifts Her collarbone
Revealing the V of Her Breasts so inviting yet alive to each
Breath
That She so softly inhales and exhales
'Hmmm'
The roundness of each breast protruding through Her bra
So inviting unashamed from Her lovers touch or just His hot
steaming stare
'Wow slow down'
'Shall I go there'
Her Abdomen creating bumps of a road that flows down into
two shapely lines

Soul of A Woman

Creative curves that are so Beautifully carved and seen
So amazingly under the tightness of Her Bodycon dress
That any man or woman would want an opportunity to pull
Her close
Just to feel the warmth of Her Breath
With an exciting desirable *'arrhhhh'*
Her hips separating creating Her pear shaped silhouette
An Apple bottom back that bounces out from the arch of Her
defined lower back
'Wait slow down am I going off Track'
Between those hips draws a V so definably deep that only a
man
Deserving of Her Love and innocence is able to stimulate
through His words
His trust
Stimulating Her Mind to connect with Her Femininity
Bringing out the Passion that Transforms Her
Arouses Her
And Pleasures Her
Her Strength comes from the roundness of Her thighs
That can hold You
Strongly Embrace You
So Lovingly Accept You
Openly invite You
Yet carry a 70kg weighted Squat making it look so Effortless
Yet weak to Your touch and caress
That's so often suppressed
Just to keep You engaged in Her Love nest
Her body is a work of art
Created for Love within and without
Not to be abused
Destroyed
Suppressed
Frozen in Shame
No one to blame but Herself
For believing societies expectation of Perfection
From a Woman
A Mother

Soul of A Woman

A Sister
A Daughter
A Partner
One day a wife
Or Her conditioning as a Child from what Her Queen Mother
Passed on
To Nurture
To Love
To Give
To Protect
To Be Strong
And always always take care of Her Appearance
The family
The home
The world
Then Herself
To stand tall
Regardless
Never to show weakness
So She always does and gives Her Best
Till one Day Her Spirit Demands for Rest
In this moment She only has Her Creators guidance
To give Her Strength
First She whispers *'I Am exhausted'*
Then She Says *'I can't do this'*
Till She shouts louder *'I lost myself'*
With Praying hands
Nothing to lose
She surrenders *'I need Your help'*
He whispers *'stop putting Your body through the test'*
Then He says *'Child it's time for rest'*
Finally shouting louder *'It's time to wake up to Your Best'*
'She Believed She Could so She Did'
Begin to get to know Her Highest SELF
By Being Self Less
She simply took the Love She always craved
Accepted She is Loved
By Her Creator

Soul of A Woman

And discovered Her Worth
So here She is
Unbreakable
Still Shakeable
Beautiful
Yet Vulnerable
Loving
Yet Humble
Graceful
Still Wonderful
Weak at times
Yet Resilient
Not fully Healed
But highly skilled
On how to care for Herself
Show Her Scars
Yet never lie
She sees Your Greatness before You do
She feels Your pain yet nourishes You
She never gives up
She is like Me
She is Like You
She is Your Spirit
Your Goddess
She is the One who sees through You

"*I Am a superwoman,
The S on my chest
signifies Strength, the
V that You visibly see
is protecting my
Vulnerability' I shed
a tear not because I've
lost but because I
gained the power and
freedom
to Be Me*"

Journey of Embracing

The fourth step is to Embrace all of Your *"Imperfections"* and know that You are imperfectly perfect. How can we begin to love ourselves or anyone else if we don't first embrace their imperfections? No one is perfect, yet many of us struggle to be *"Perfect"*. This desire to be perfect almost destroyed me. As a Personal Trainer my desire for the 'Perfect Body' gave way to so much negativity, expectations, limitations, restrictions and obsessions that led to a very negative body image called 'Body Dysmorphia'. **Body dysmorphic disorder (BDD), or body dysmorphia is a mental health condition where a person spends a lot of time worrying about flaws in their appearance. These flaws are often unnoticeable to others, yet can lead to depression, anxiety, self-harm and suicidal thoughts.**

Whilst I was building the *"Perfect Figure Model Body"* I was losing the real essence of life, *"Balance"*. I wanted so badly to have the compliments, look amazing in tight dresses and achieve this sculpted *"5 star physique"* that my perception of *"Perfection"* meant *"Obsession"*. See I am one person that does not like rules from others. Yet I thought I could handle placing rules on myself? Wrong.

The more rules I placed on myself the more of the inner child in me screamed. I remember when I was little. I had to complete my maths homework. Mum had left me and my older brother to finish it alone, with no guidance. She said once You finish You can come and join me to play outside. It was a warm summer's day. My brother never listened to my mum and I'm sure He didn't do it right but He finished and left me alone. My desire to have it *"Perfect"* so mum would be pleased with me kept me stuck in the chair, frustrated, alone to sort it out myself. I cried so much until a neighbour knocked on the door and helped me to finish it. I don't remember my childhood years much, however I remember this moment like it was yesterday. So placing rules on myself to be *"Perfect"* is like reliving that moment but this time I had to do it myself as I'm an adult now *"a Mother"* so I had to figure it out alone, so I thought.

So when I became *"Depressed"* I automatically believed I had to overcome this alone. After all I had done everything myself right? Again Wrong.

Our old conditioning from childhood will continuously be re-lived subconsciously if we don't heal that part of ourselves. The deep work is required and this is why these 5 steps have to be done. We are on the fourth so only one more to go.

Reflection

To Embrace myself I had to face me. Look within. My values, who I aspire to be. What message did I want to pass onto my daughter about Loving ourselves and *"Body Image"*. Was perfection really necessary to make me Happy? No. I had to care less about my body and more about living my life regardless of how I felt and looked. I just had to Embrace Me. So that's where Acceptance, Letting Go, Forgiveness had to occur for me to be here. To Love I must first be willing to Embrace all that I am. And be happy to be *'Imperfectly Perfect Me'*. Are You ready to embark on this journey with me? It's going to get a little more personal. However this is where You *"Empower Yourself"* and really set Yourself FREE.

Exercise 1

Centering Exercise

Take 5 Deep breaths through Your nose and out Your mouth and repeat *'I AM CALM, I AM PRESENT, I ACCEPT MYSELF, I LET GO, I FORGIVE MYSELF, I AM WILLING TO EMBRACE ME....*

The Mirror Exercise

All You need is the willingness to do this exercise and a full length mirror.

Upon waking up is the best time when you are alone in your overwhelmed thoughts.

Take off every item of clothing. If this seems too much at first You can stay fully clothed for now, and as you continue to practice this daily remove an item of clothing.

Be gentle with yourself this one takes time, Love and patience.

Look at the area of Your body You are fixated with the most/don't like. Just like the poem on Self-Love begin to send this area Love. Add a small touch and embrace it, breathe, then slowly move to the other areas of your body repeating the same thing. Uncomfortable right? No one teaches us how to Love ourselves, let alone our bodies so this is very deep inner work.

HOW CAN YOU EXPECT SOMEONE ELSE TO LOVE YOUR MIND AND BODY IF YOU DO NOT LOVE YOURSELF?

Heart Exercise

Take a moment after you have finished. Allow your emotions to be, don't suppress instead be *"STILL"* and really feel them. Place Your hand on your heart and repeat the centering exercise. Then ask yourself *'What do I need right now'* and listen. Your body will talk back to you. Now it will constantly desire nurturing. This is now where your self-care list kicks in. Do 3 things daily that you Love and aim to do one a day, if you can do more *'just do it'*.

Exercise 2

In your Journal write a list of things that You Love to do. No matter how small or big. Don't reach for ones requiring money, there are plenty you can do at home daily. Let your imagination run wild.

Pick 3 a day. Make it a practice of doing them daily. You are already doing the Daily and Evening Ritual so that's already some to add to your list. Add a few more. From this picture below.

Embracing and
Expressing Your
Feelings will set
you FREE.

Free2Embraceme

"The Queen in You is Rising, Beautiful It's time to pick up Your Crown"

Own Your Inner Diva

Tiredness brings back darkness in Light
Brings sadness in Happiness
Keeping me frozen in a web of lies and Imperfection
Why is the world full of condemnation born from suppression
Causing depression
Why do others perception of You become their own isolation
Causing anger
Bitterness hate and even confusion
We're born from Love yet we learn to hate
We're born for Greatness yet we play small
Because we fear the unknown
Destroy those who Uplift us
Those who are Rising yet suffering
So You want to make them Feel guilty for Growing
Developing
Elevating and Encouraging You
Look within what You lack
Failing to see that the mirror of You has Your back
They see Your Worth
Your True Potential
They go harder on You
Because they know
Behind that pain
Lies a True Diamond
Who is made of Love and Passion
Their words will hurt
To bring out the pain
Guiding You to Dance in the rain
Unleashing the Goddess that You're afraid to see
Stop the running
Stop the pretence
Stop acting like You *'Got it all'*
Be True to who You are
The Bigger the Rise the harder the fall
Own up to Your Inner diva

Soul of A Woman

It's time to look in the mirror
Naked and Strong
Get back Your Strength
Take one step forward into the place that You Belong

"To Embrace Your flaws is a skill

To Love Yourself is the magic pill"

I Am that I Am

Who Am I
I reside in a temple I call my Body
I breathe in the air of life
I walk in a path with an endless road
I see through eyes of Divinity
Yet I still do not know Me
I was born out of Love
Taken from a man's rib
Carved so carefully and Beautifully
Yet I do not Love Me
My Mother lovingly carried me in Her womb
Protected me from a world that constantly tried to put Her
down and abuse Her
She suffered so I wouldn't
She gave so I never lacked
She Nurtured me so I could Grow
She gave up Her Life for Me
Yet I allow Myself and others to destroy Me
Her wounds are so deep
That She hides them from Me
Just so I can gain the Strength to be
Be strong for my Child
Hide my pain so She can feel safe
'No I won't hide anymore'
I will show my own that life is a journey so challenging at
times
Hateful
Full of negativity and pain
However She can be whoever She desires to be
Not what society says She should be
I will show Her it's ok to break down and not know it all
Or control it all or carry any pain alone
Just so She can protect Her own
Still I have to set myself Free so She can be Free
I have to be Self Less to Her and to others

Soul of A Woman

STOP thinking of what the world perceives a Mother should be
'NO I Am not Perfect'
'YES I Am a Superwoman'
And *'YES I need to be nurtured too'*
Before I was *'Mummy'* and carried Her in my tummy
I was careless
Fun
Creative
Bold
Independent
Sexy
Sassy
Cool
Vibrant
FREE
'I'm sorry Angel it's time for Mummy to be Me'
'Who Am I'
A Woman
'What do I Desire'
Love
'Who can Heal Me'
The Goddess in Me
'When is the right time'
Now
'How do I begin'
By saying *'YES I Am Worthy'*
'I Am breaking the chains'
My Queen carried from generation to generation
'I Am accepting where I Am'
'I Am God's Greatest Creation'
'I Am connecting Spiritually'
In His Image
Like a butterfly
Floating slowly and Beautifully
Through a journey of healing
'I AM A QUEEN'

"As I discovered Me.
I uncovered the Greatest Gift I have for my "Self" daily. I am Free to be unapologetically Imperfectly Perfect Me"

Life Begins

As I enter my 40s
Life begins
I've cried many tears
Faced many fears
Thought I would never smile or Love again
Sunshine blinded by darkness
Surrounded by my Loved ones yet clouded by own loneliness
In my Mind full of pain
I lost myself
Emptiness became my morning shower of rain
I wanted to end the suffering
I wanted to feel better today
A voice whispered lovingly
'Have patience my Love'
That was my message from High Above
'I have Faith in You'
That was my message from deep within
I said *'YES I want to thrive'*
Detaching my conscious need to survive
I began to Accept Me
Discover Me
Love Me
In return God bought Me You
He whispered loudly
'Spread Love and pass on Your teachings'
'How' I asked
'Just be You' He whispered
I asked myself *'How can I inspire others and end their
Suffering?'*
'Use Your voice'
So I made a choice
To simply overflow my cup and spill it over You All
That is how my Life began
And that my friend
Became my Purpose

Soul of A Woman

My Calling
My reason for the suffering
Became my reason to Live again

"*I raise my voice because it heals Me, I raise it louder so You can heal You*"

Life is Like a Box of Chocolates

Life is like a box of chocolates
'You never know what You're gonna get'
It's a Gift with many goodies
It comes with many treats
Given graciously by a Loved one
Or even given by You to You
To simply comfort and indulge You
Making You feel pleasured
Warm
Tingling
Giddy
Appreciated
Celebrated
Naughty yet nice
It is one of Life's guilty Pleasures
Melting slowly in Your mouth
Causing You to heighten Your senses
Creating yet healing Your emotions
Providing Love
Comfort
Calmness and even serenity
It comes in many shapes
Colours
Flavours
Textures
You open the box
Your eyes create an image with a sense of Gratitude
A feeling of Excitement
For what You are about to indulge so Pleasurably
You make a choice
Not really knowing what it tastes or feels like
Yet it looks pretty to Your mind's eye
Above the chocolates You have the ingredients of what each
chocolate has inside
Mouth-watering for that first Satisfying lick or bite

Soul of A Woman

Your senses heighten
Your saliva elevates
Mouth open
Chocolate touches Your lips
Tongue
Eagerly
Impatiently
You take that first bite
'Yuck'
'It's too rich'
Too dark
Too sweet
You've been mislead
That was not worth the wait
Or that hungry bite
You made that choice
No one to blame
You choose another chocolate
It's just a game
Do You continue eating it
Or spit it out
You have the Power
It's in Your mouth
Curse all You want
Shout all You want
Continue to taste its richness and let Your senses shut down
Just because You don't want to waste it
Or know Yourself and what You like
And choose to spit it out
Take another bite
This time a different chocolate
Read the ingredients carefully
Do not be fooled
By how pretty and smooth it looks
Decide to become familiar with the ingredients
Bringing an image of what You Desire
Forget the bitterness of the bite You took before
That's in the past

Soul of A Woman

'Let it go'
Be Mindful that the Present is in Your hands
This Gift so loving and so Divine
Is in Your Power
In Your Mind
Wonderfully prepared
Packaged and presented to bring Happiness into Your life
Now grab it Gratefully
Put it in Your mouth
Slowly
Let Your senses enlighten Graciously
Let it melt into Your tongue
Patiently
Do not be greedy or rush the process
This feeling so Pleasurable
So Orgasmic
So Serene
Is here to stay if You allow Yourself to Simply be
Be in the Present
Mindfully
Keep it slowly melting
Tasting
Discovering
Indulging
Guilt-Free
Feel what it does to every part of Your body
Senselessly
Taste
Touch
Sound
Colours
This feeling can last for hours
You have a whole box to Discover
Wonderfully
Just decide to be Patient with Your choices
Remembering that every chocolate is Unique
Each piece has a different taste
Even when You know every ingredient

Soul of A Woman

Sometimes You may not be ready for its taste
'Life is like a box of chocolates'
It really is Your choice to make
'You never know what You're gonna get'
It's not a game or a simple bet
It's a Creation of what You like
What You Desire
What You are Worthy of
What You wish to Invest
What You Decide to Believe
What You Focus on
It simply is 2 choices You can make
1 To choose the wrong chocolate just because it's pretty yet
Became bitter
2 To choose the right chocolate because it's rough and
becomes Stronger
'Life is like a box of chocolates'
It's such a Gift
Carefully Created
Packaged and prepared with goodies
Tangy
Bitter
Tasty
Sweet
'You never know what You're gonna get'
So I chose to discover it's many Pleasures and Wondrous Gifts
Life simply is Yours to Create
'So Simply Decide to make it Great'

"*Life isn't about finding Yourself Life is about Re- inventing Yourself*"

Life is Like a box
of Chocolates.
You never know
what you're gona
Get.

Free2embraceme

Who Am I?

My name is Neusa Catoja

Natural   Caring

Empowering   Alluring

Unique   Tenacious

Sincere   Omnificent

Amazing   Joyful

                 Ambitious

I Am the light that shines so bright
I Am the one who won the fight
I Am the friend that You desire
I Am the voice born to Inspire
I Am a woman full of Grace
I Am a warrior of life who won the race
I Am made of Love and full of Passion
I came into this world to fulfil my Mission
To uplift Queens who will raise and support their Kings
Protect their Princesses to become Queens
To see their worth and their inner Beauty
To Light the world and end the pain
To remind You that Your suffering was not in vain

Now it's time for you to write your own Poem and Name. Use words that empower you, uplift you and symbolise your unique characteristics.

Who Am I?

My Name is_____

First Name   Surname

Write your own *'I Am Poem'*. Make it beautiful, make it amazing, use your imagination bring yourself into this present moment, like a child let your own imagination run wild. Use some of your affirmations.

I Am

....

....

....

....

....

....

....

....

....

....

....

....

....

....

....

At Peace with Now

As I sit in bed
A sense of calmness
Gratitude
Serenity Embraces Me
I pinch myself just to see if I'll wake up from what feels like a
path of Love and Peace
Two years ago an overwhelming exhaustion
Anger
Oppression filled with confusion
Hatred towards Myself
Because I had forgotten what it felt like to be Me
I often wished I could sleep and not wake up to a darkness
that became my morning
Afternoon and evening sadness
Still I always woke up to the same negativity that took away
My tranquillity that became my Sanctuary
I speak of a girl once lost in a world She Created that meant
She had to be Perfect to the world just because society said as
a Mother She has to be
She felt like a failure to Her Creation
She became so disconnected from the Love She once felt for
Herself
So how could She Love Her own child
When She's under a dark cloud of insecurity
She had to fall so She could begin to heal from the wounds
That Her Queen Mother suppressed in order to protect
Her Family
So they wouldn't suffer under the arms of a man who was
meant to protect them with Love
This girl was stubborn
When others advised
Suggested
Or tried to guide Her to do things medically
She remembered the calmness

Soul of A Woman

Faith
Strength
And Persistence Her Queen Mother had that one day would
ignite Her own purpose to...
One day set Her mind Free
Faith the size of a mustard seed was ignited by
Her Queen Mother who prayed every night
For Her child to one day truly see
That She is the root of the Family
The one who connected the dots from the flaws that Her
Family kept so secretly
She knew no one is Perfect
So why should She be
No Her pain was not in vain
She woke up from a whole so deep
So dark that even a fly on a wall would crumble and fall just
From the sight of the anger
She inflicted on Herself because She felt all Love was lost
So frustration became Her comfortability
NO
'Not this girl'
She made a choice and took full Responsibility
That girl is Me
I Accepted where I was
I took full blame for allowing my thoughts to Create a Vision
That was planted by a word from a Doctor labelling Me
'Depressed'
Yes I believed He was right
I Accepted His diagnosis
BUT I refused to accept that a tiny white sugar coated tiny
Substance made of chemicals
Manufactured by man would eventually put the pieces of my
Mind together and fix Me
So that the next check up by another Doctor would label Me
'Happy'
'Really'
That is so bloody Hilarious

Soul of A Woman

If I wanted a happy pill I would search online and order a pill
labelled *'Ecstasy'*
Or even call my girl and ask Her for some weed
Because that will make Me *'Happy'* instantly
Yet the Doctor and label on the box's side effects said clearly
'This medication may cause serious suicidal thoughts
Sleeplessness
Anxiety'
Why would I want to change my current label *'depressed'* to...
'Suicidal...anxious...insomniac...'
Someone please You might as well call me
'Clinically depressed maniac'
I took tiny little steps
Focussed on my Values
Began to talk myself from *'depressed'* to *'self-expressed'*
I wrote when I couldn't speak
I danced when I couldn't cry
I let the tears I suppressed
Lift the weight off my chest
I simply let my emotions be
I Let go of the guilt that I carried from the first time He angrily
shouted *'You broke our family'*
NO
He no longer had a hold on Me
I began to see my SELF as a Strong Vulnerable Child of God
Natural
Empowered
Unique
Sexy
Amazing
I stared at my reflection in the mirror
Naked
Vulnerable
Unashamed
And for the first time
I saw a Spiritual *'Being'*
I started to be kind to Myself and discover this body is so Sexy
Carved so Graciously

Soul of A Woman

I unapologetically spoke my Truth and shut down all those
Haters...bullies...takers...unbelievers...jealous...
Judgemental...fake...energy vampires and users
I began to give Myself what I lacked for years and expected
others to give Me
Yet felt disappointed by what I saw in the movies
Wasn't real Love
I began to Love Me
As a result I attracted my Soul Mate
My Lover
My Best Friend
My King
The one who Guides
Encourages Me yet Challenges Me to be the Best that I can be
I finally Embraced all my Imperfections and realised that
'I Am Imperfectly Perfect Me'
Gratitude saved Me
It's my morning coffee
Fills Me up with Excitement
Reminds Me to Smile
'I Am grateful I Am Alive'
Gratitude is now my Greatest Altitude
My Lover and Guide
Abundantly Blessing Me with more little Gifts and Wonders
So Precious and Beautiful
So that's why Forever
'I Am Grateful'

"No matter how little You have, be Grateful, Gratitude is Your Greatest Altitude"

How Does it Feel to Be Free

As the darkness becomes light
A sweet morning stretch and Excitement engulfs Me
I smile to myself as my arms wider than branches from a tree
Lengthening so quickly as my sweet voice whispers
'Thank You God I Am alive I Am Free'
Like a Child Excitedly rushes to Her Mother's arms to receive
that familiar loving scent and warmth generated from Her
Nurturer's chest She holds on whispering
'Mummy I love You'
But this time my nurturer
My Protector
The Love that I feel is inside of Me
I hug myself and give Thanks for awakening into a Spiritual
Realm that is so Unique
Yet Adventurous to Me
It's like I woke from a deep automatic
Systematic out of sync
Controlled
Egoistic
Discriminative
Restricted prison
That I thought was how life was meant to be
Work a 9-5
Pay My bills
Take care of My Child
Be the EVERYTHING She and others expect Me to be
'Nah Sah that ain't Me'
I Am Unique
I Am Stubborn
I Am Destined for Greatness
I Am the Conductor of my own Destiny
I Woke to the Truth
My own Reality
Where Freedom of Speech allows Me to be
Unapologetically Raw

Soul of A Woman

Real without holding back
Just because You don't like what I see
'Does what I say cause anxiety'
*'Does my rawness make You think that You are Better off
alone'*
Guess it's safer to keep me out of sight
Because You think my words will hurt or bite
You are Your own worst enemy
I Am the Diamond that You chose to crush
I Am the friend who came to give You a push
I Am the Faith that You can Trust
After so much pain and destruction that Your Mind Body and
Spirit endured
Isolated in hatred that You once looked Beautiful
And now You are lost and confused that the Beauty You saw is
so far from what You see
Staring back at You
This is Me
I came so You can see that claiming Your Freedom
You're right to Speak up
So You can finally Heal from the wounds they or even You
inflicted within and without
I know Your Greatness before Your Forgiveness
'Can I fix You'
'NO'
I just simply give You the tools and guidance once You say
'I Am Worthy'
Acceptance is Life's Essence
Letting go is Liberating
Forgiveness is key
Embracing is Allowing
Self-Love is Healing
And Discovering these Wonders of Dreams filled with bubbles
And colours so warm
Yet Self-Love can also bring on Emotions that knock at Your
door
Just to create the fire that bring You back to Reality
Reality is here in the Present

Soul of A Woman

Yet Your Mind has the Power to Create an Imagination of a
Life that You Desire
Mixed with Goals and simple steps to manifest *YOUR* Future
Freedom is Feeling Ready
Excited
Empowered
Desired
Omnificent
Mindful
Present
Calm
Beautiful
Liberated
Amazing
Joyful
Loved
This is what it Feels to be Free
In Your Mind You have the ability to attract what You lack and
Guide Your own Self-Love Journey
In this Journey no matter what the storm may bring
*'I Am fully protected with Love for Myself guided by Angels
who have never left Me
'Yes I Am Free'*

I Rise, Together We Rise

You lay awake senselessly
Silence has become a part of You
Yet there is so much noise
How can a silent night scream so endlessly
Anxiety has become Your closest Friend
Protecting You yet making You afraid
Afraid to leave Your house yet afraid to return to a place
You once felt safe
It's not Your body not even Your Mind
Happiness is just a past left behind
A past so hard to reach
So impossible to touch
To Feel
So exhaustive to even Smile
'Why…
When…
How'
So many questions not even a simple answer
Do You give up
Or do You get up
Choices are so hard to make
You don't even want to hurt anymore
Don't want to hurt Your Loved ones
So You fight
Pretend
Put on Your mask
Fake Smile
Slowly dying inside
'Why Me'
Slow Breath
Fast Breath
No Breath
Silence
'STOP'

Soul of A Woman

You want to scream so loud
Yet no one can hear You shout
'What's the point'
Scream now
Slow down
Be Calm
Be Still
Be Strong
Don't listen to the voice of doubt
Listen to the One who knows You deep down
Release the tears
Face Your fears
Breathe
Head up
Fake it till You make it
Smile
Whisper
'I Am safe'
'I Am Strong'
'Today I Rise'
Wait I said it, so it is true
'I Am Strong'
'I Am still here'
'I didn't give up'
Another step
You move forward
You say it
You are living it
'I fell'
'Now I Rise'
Take a deep long Purifying Breath
You Begin to Create Your Life force
Your world
Your *'Being'*
'YES You are in control of Your Destiny'
'Accept it'
'Let it go'
'Forgive'

Soul of A Woman

'Embrace'
'Love'
Breathe
Live
'Yes I Rise'
'I Rise, Together We Rise'

I Smile

With every breath I awaken
Thoughtless disturbance comes to me
Why does the anger You suppress want to destruct Me like a
magnet that no longer has the Strength or Power
Your reflection in the mirror
Is Your own perception
So why do You choose to show Your Imperfection
Do You not see that I breathe so Peacefully with Serenity
With a Smile that Vibrates through My Being to the Life that
You've been Living
Your silence is so loud
Yet my song *'I Smile'* in My head over and over Peacefully
Feeling so Proud
I've died of the ego
I've locked my past in a box
It often says hello for a minute
Awakening Feelings that caused me to hide from my
Authenticity
My song becomes louder *'I Smile'*
Then that Feeling disappears as fast as it comes whilst I say
'Goodbye'
Don't worry I will still *'Smile'* cause my expression of
Contentment in My face whilst You crave for a reaction of
Destruction to end the frustration
That You Feel from Your pain
Yet You get no reaction
Doesn't mean I don't care
Doesn't mean I don't hurt cause You hurt
It just means that I've learnt to Protect my Energy so I can
increase my Synergy
Yet *'I smile'*
'I'm just simply Being Me'

Love

Love Is more than a word
Overused
Underrated
Often confused
Painful at times and so abused
A four letter word that has more Power than any nuclear
Weapon
So destructive
Complicated
Unexpected
Yet Liberating
It's our Natural born right
It creeps up on You
Without Care or fears
Many times bringing Joy
Through its challenge
Many tears
We fight to get it
We fight to keep it
We fight to end it
We Live by it
With it
Even against it
Often run from it
Deny it
Yet Pray for it
So why is it simple yet hard
To Love ourselves
To Nurture ourselves
To Care for ourselves
Knowing how to Love others without conditions
Yet placing conditions on ourselves
We crave Love
Work towards Trust
Give with no expectations

Soul of A Woman

Jumping through many relations
How can we give others what we do not have for ourselves
What others see is our reflection of what they lack
'It's time to get our Own Loving back'

Fear of Love

Blinded by my own tears
Not knowing what to do
Afraid of letting go
Too close to take it slow
'I know where I Desire to be'
'I know where I Feel Safe'
'So why does my Heart Feel so heavy'
'Yet Light when You're near'
Feeling Amazing at times
Yet so lonely at break of day
Isolated by fears
Soaked in my own tears
Your intentions are Loving
Yet Your speech is so cold
Patience and Compassion
Lives in Me
Driving our connection into a deep Passion
Our hearts desire each other
Yet our Spirit screams for Freedom
We are so close
Yet so far
Together in Love
Yet so distant by hate
We lose Hope daily
For those we once Loved
Love is our greatest Healer
It's the reason we are here
'Yet we choose to hurt each other'
Seeking what was once our past
Why do we neglect what is meant to be
Due to fear that it's happening too fast
The past has hurt us badly
Our Present is full of Beautiful Surprises
We know our future is as One
Forgiveness is key

Soul of A Woman

We wait Patiently
In fear that it's too late
To give Love one more Chance
We seek what we often lack for Ourselves
The Freedom to Love Endlessly
Seek this Internal Love that's within
Once we connect Spiritually towards a Journey to Self-Love
Only then can we truly be open
To giving it to one another

Reflection

As I reflect on my Life
As the rain so easily pours
My Life has been a rollercoaster
One I share so openly
Not to boast
But simply to toast
That Life is simply a river that flows
Often bumping into rocks
Flowing fast and slow
Freely moving Endlessly
Mindlessly out of control
Till it comes to a Calm after a Storm
Only to return back into a Storm
Life simply is a Journey of constant flow
When it rains it really pours
Reminding You to be Still
Slow down and just be
Be Free to choose Your currency
Design Your Destiny

Soul of A Woman

Just be Mindful that there are times You cannot choose where
You will end up
Just like a river it never stops
Until You do
It Beautifully flows with excitement and wonder
With no Destiny
Take the same way
Without guilt
Regret or blame
Be prepared for a bumpy ride
Never put the breaks on for too long
Or You will miss out on Your next ride
Board Your ship
Put Your life coat on
Strap it tight and take a big long breath in
Ommmmmmm
Hold it
Be Still
Smile
Breathe out long
Haaaaaaahhhhhhh
Put Your seatbelt on
'IT'S GONNA BE A BUMPTY YET EXCITING RIDE'

A Journey to Self-Love

Well Done Beautiful for getting to the last step. The fifth step that connects this journey. Remember we don't aim to reach the Destination. We aim to walk on a continuous path of Self-Love.

Therefore what we have done from the very beginning has to be a constant flow and a daily practice. We are always evolving, changing and growing.

As we peel one layer another one comes through. Learning to cater to each one is what I call a *"Process"*. Trust this process and be Patient with Yourself. Healing takes time.

I never knew I didn't Love myself enough therefore I gave my time, last money I had and my all to those I Loved, even those I just met. It's in my nature to automatically look at someone with trust and if they confide in me my mind races with seeking answers for them. This very nature serves me graciously yet many times depleted me.

My vulnerability was my weakness to many, because I saw it that same way. Until I realised that my vulnerability is my greatest strength it's a beautiful part of me. I Loved before, I will Love again and I will always continue to give Love. However I have learnt that my cup has to be overflowing first before I give. That applies to every area of my life. Emotionally, Physically and Spiritually in Mind Body and Spirit I have learnt that I matter first.

As women we are taught to care and nurture and be the head of the household (*no it's not men, whoever said that is delusional*). Our homes function when everything is in order.

We have been conditioned by our Ancestors to carry their chains often referred to as *"Generational curses"*. This dates back to the slavery days. We still carry the slave mentality in us. Serving others first before we care for our own needs. Back then our freewill was taken from us. Now we are free to make choices as to whether we stay imprisoned in our minds or we break down the chains and set ourselves free.

I started with my voice. You can too. I asked for a guide, He was within me already. I connected with my own Spiritual Goddess Being within me as I asked it Why? Many times yet no answers came.

I had faith so I asked for more Faith, I got it.

I was sick and exhausted, I asked for rest I got it.

When it all got too much I simply prayed out loud *'God I don't care what is happening to me, please bless me so I can bless others'*. My answer was to 'Love Myself First' and I do.

There are no exercises to this journey, you've done them all. Yet some of us have deeper work to do that may need a Guide, A life Coach, someone who will listen isn't always enough.

In order to *"Transform"* we must be willing to do the work, and be held accountable for our actions so they get done. Because when You Decide to Change and say *'YES I Am Worthy'* you will be faced with many challenges.

Family, friends, clients all coming at you demanding to keep you still and with them. Not that they don't want to see You Elevate but because they are used to the old you.

Some are just concerned and want to keep you safe, others just want what they want. I told my daughter the other day *'Babygirl everyone is Selfish, and so they should be'*, however we must begin to be *"Self-Less"*, it simply means, giving more to ourselves first'. In this lifetime everyone wants something for themselves and it's right that they should. Everyone is striving for Importance and a Purpose if they haven't yet found it. The secret is that they already have their purpose inside them.

Love is the purpose we all want to feel. When you feel this Love, You do more of what makes You feel that Love and that's where Your Gift is born. Your own *"Self-Expression"* will heal the *"Depression"* and allow you to connect with the things you Love most, beginning with *"YOU"*.

I Love people, my family, friends, nature, dance, poetry, a gift I only uncovered within as I worked on the 5 steps I list in this journal, inspiring others, talking and Loving. The more I expressed the more I let go.

My circle of friends became smaller, giving less to others and more to me became my remedy, moving my body and connecting spiritually with meditation yoga and dance empowered me.

I became the person I've always had within me. No magic pill did that. I am the magic pill I just needed guidance, something *"Greater"* than me to guide me and Love me unconditionally. *'Me and my Goddess within'*. We are *"One"* there is no separation, *'My God lives inside Me'*.

I used to repeat this daily bible verse **'God is within Her She will not fall, He will Help Her at break of Day'** Psalm 45:5. I repeat verses in the bible when I need spiritual strengthening from my Creator. He knew me before I was even born so there is no way He will ever let me fall.

So if you have fallen it's not because you are any different from me. You are a reflection of me. Where You were I once was and can often go back there when my soul needs feeding again with self-love and self-care, however I'm now equipped with my Angels, my Spiritual guides, my Goddess and internal guide.

My body always talks back to me when I am disconnected spiritually so I reconnect again with *"Gratitude"* and *"Faith"*.

I now believe that *"IMPOSSIBLE"* is a word put together with one letter missing, 'A'. *"IMPOSSIBLE"* reads *"I 'AM' POSSIBLE"*. I also wanted to be *"PERFECT"* and whilst I felt *"IMPERFECT"* I was, as this word also missed the same letter 'A'. *'I AM PERFECT'*, in my Creator's eye *'I AM'* the most *'PERFECT'* thing on this earth, I was created with so much Love and so are You. You see now how words are so powerful? And how *"MAGNIFICENT"* we really are?

Self Love is key to Happiness

Free2embraceme

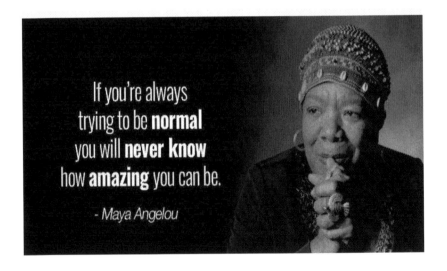

If you're always trying to be **normal** you will **never know** how **amazing** you can be.

- Maya Angelou

Changes

Upon the rays of the sun it's heat slowly awakening
Burning through glass
So Vibrant
So Bright
It's constantly shining
No matter the seasons
Appearing so effortlessly for many reasons
A constant reminder
That You're *'Alive'*
A daily alarm that needs no setting
All it takes is for You to open Your eyes
To see its Energy
To see You Smile and whisper softly
'I Am grateful for another day'
Monday it's Motivating
Tuesday it's Trusting
Wednesday it's Whispering
Or even Wicked
Just to come out to Play and Laugh a little
Thursday it's throwing back as a reminder to get back on track
Friday it's FREEDOM
Because the weekend is near
Saturday it's Sassy
An occasion to be informal or even classy
It's Your choice so choose wisely
Sunday it's Blessed
Abundantly Soul Searching
You made it through another week
It's always appearing with many changes
Bringing You many choices
You will always get another chance to start again
So begin to see
How You Embrace the Sun
It's colours change as You close Your eyes
You see a rainbow without the rain

Soul of A Woman

So many vibrant colours yet Your eyes are shut
Begin to open them get through the dark
Start with Gratitude
Let it be Your Greatest Altitude
See how it changes You
How it Embraces You
How it hugs You...
'IT'S TIME TO LEVEL UP'

"When You change the way You look at things, the things You look at Change"

Dr Wayne Dyer

I have learnt

That through this Journey of Self Love
I am Unique
Alone in my Own childlike Imagination in Contentment of the
words I Speak
I am not a superhero
Nor am I a body
I am Divinely Gracefully carved and sculpted
Beautifully with the finest lines
I Am a Spirit full of Love
A Goddess Protected by Angels from High Above
God knew what He Created was placed on this earth to Win
To cry a river
Climb the Highest mountain
To Live everyday like it was the last
To give Selflessly with no expectations
To Love Unconditionally with so much Passion
To learn to Dance in the rain
And very often feel pain
To not be ashamed of who *'I Am'*
Or hold onto what others did or hold onto blame
To not feel guilt for things I could've done
Instead be glad that I moved on
To let people go
Circumstances flow
Yet continue to Shine and Grow
To find Peace within
To Live a Life of Discovery
To step in fear
Yet still have Faith
That He is near
And will never let Me fall
Every piece He carved has a Purpose in this Life
My scars
My curves
My cellulite

Soul of A Woman

My kinky afro hair
My nose
My lips
My Beautiful soft brown skin
He Blessed them all
He named Me
His *'African Queen'*
With Love for my *'King'*
Who sees my Worth as *'A Queen'*
With Love for Me who Loves and gives so Graciously
With Love for my Creation who sees a Mother's Unconditional
Nurturing Presence
She is my Princess soon to become *'A Queen'*
With Love for my Mother who raised me and Ignited the
Diamond within
Her Prayers Saved Me
I am now passing on EVERYTHING God has equipped Me with
So She can see that Life is indeed *'like a box of chocolates'*
Sometimes bitter
Sometimes sweet
Yet She has a choice of which one She Desires to pick
God is Love
Our Inner Guide
Listen to the words He Speaks
'Don't feel ashamed to cry'
Wipe the tears with Pride
This path of Self Discovery is so Amazing
Breath-taking
Worth every tear
Every scar
Every *'No'*
It's Unique to You
Just remember
There is a much *'Bigger Force within You'*
Call it *'God'*
'Allah'
'Most High'
'Jehovah'

Soul of A Woman

'Yahweh'
It's one Force that is a *"Higher Essence"* of You
But You must be Willing to throw Yourself into its Mercy with
Trust that You will *'Be ok'*
One must fall to Wake up to *'SELF'*
To know their own Strength and Discover their Greatest Gifts
To give Love and receive Love
Is Your Highest intention
To share these Gifts with the world to make a difference
Save a Life
Make someone Smile
'Be the change You wish to see'
Throw Yourself into His arms
Discover Your Destiny
'Breathe'
'Let Go'
'Embrace'
'Love the Beauty within You'
'Be Free'
'We are all Connected in the Great Circle of Life'

As You Ask so Shall You Receive

I asked for Strength
He made Me weak
I asked to be heard
He told Me to speak
I asked for a challenge
He showed Me depression
I asked for a Gift
He Guided Me towards Self-Expression
I asked for a Friend
He bought Me You
I asked for Love
He taught Me how
I asked to Bless others
He gave Me this Gift
This Gift was always within Me
Imprisoned by My Mind
Lying dormant yet ready to Shine
Now I Thank Him daily for His Protection and Wisdom
Guiding Me towards my Own Self-Healing Journey
A Journey so bitter and dark
That led me to a Journey so Sweet and Light
I now know I never walked alone
Physically I do
I take Care of my Creation and Me
Often allowing others to shower Me with Love
Yet Spiritually I Am never alone
I walk by Faith
Never by sight
I'll walk this same road again
Just because I know I can
Yet know that next time this path will be different
As I walk with Self-Love
God's Love
Universal Love
And as I ask for more Love

Soul of A Woman

Patiently
Graciously
Gratefully
Unconditionally
Yet unexpectedly
He gives Me more
Knowing I will never close my door
To the truth that He exists
He is a Power I cannot resist
Nor deny
Suppress or neglect
You see non-Believer
God is not some Man
Above the clouds
He does not Live in the alter
He is a part of You
A part of Me
All Creative
All Powerful
All Beautiful
All Loving
And Unique
God is Black
God is White
He looks like You
And looks like Me
Limitless
Omnificent
An Energy so Irresistible
His Presence to intense
When we Connect in silence
In Meditation
In Prayer
With Faith
That which we ask for in His Name
We Receive

Therefore I tell You, whatever You ask for in prayer, believe that You have received it, and it will be Yours.

Matthew 11:24

The Secret

As She Woke from a dark destructive Self-loathing past
Believing that this Feeling was here to last
She was clueless to what a Journey to *'One SELF'* would ever
Feel like
Her need to Feel
To want to Love
Was all She ever needed
A tug so tight corrupted Her Mind
A Faith the size of a mustard Seed
Whispered *'I can do this on my own'* Uplifted Her spirit yet
diminished what they said
'You are depressed and a pill will fix You'
A whisper so loud screamed at Her Mind and attacked Her
exhaustive body
Reminding Her that only She will know how
She had to breakdown before She could crawl
Die to Herself so She could spread Her wings
Emerge like a butterfly floating senselessly
To learn to be Grateful for the smallest of things
To see Beauty in a leaf
Colours in Beautiful flowers
To Feel the energy of the earth grounding Her Safely with both
feet
One foot forward and another She Rose
Took one step after another with Faith and Determination
that She would one day Win the race
Face up to Her Fears
Let go of the need to hide behind Her pain and Her warm
tears
Accept that Life can be Simple once She Allows
Allows Herself to be
Like a bird and Raise those Beautiful wings to the world
Yet to those who doubted
Rise like a Phoenix leaving flames like a Trailblazer
So those who don't Hear Her Feel Her Presence

Soul of A Woman

'This girl is on Fire'
She burned out all the negativity
All the doubts She took on
Traced Her fingers through every scar as a symbol that She has
come so far
She hasn't even started
Yet Her Movement is Guarded
Protected by Angels
Embraced by Her Inner Goddess
'What secret does She possess'
Now that She stopped putting Her body to the test
Lovingly let Her Mind rest
If You don't know take Her hand
See the Vision She Birthed to never let no Woman or Feminine
Goddess be suppressed
To no longer Live a Life of stress
To Accept that Life's Journey can often be challenging yet
every time we open our eyes we are
'BLESSED'
Blessed to see another day
'Guess what it is Yours to Embrace'
To be Grateful that in every little Breath we take we get
another Chance to start over
To take one more step
Maybe do that one thing You thought You couldn't do
Because You placed so many limitations and restrictions to
what once Felt good
Now it Feels so bad
Guilt creeps in
Tomorrow is not guaranteed
Only today
Ask Yourself daily
'What is the worst that could happen if I just let go'
The result is that You will be *'FREE'*
Free from limitations and expectations that You have placed
on Yourself
The need for perfection has disconnected You from what's
real

Soul of A Woman

It's time to stop the self-destruction that causes confusion
that came to steal Your Passion
Let's begin to really Feel
Feel Good when You Laugh
Feel Good when You Wake up
Feel Good when You Love
Feel Good because You can
A Feeling is something You get to choose
'What do You really have to lose'
You have already lost the old *'SELF'*
Let's begin to Discover the Newness that's *'You'*
It's not going to be easy my Dear
It's gonna be bumpy
It's gonna be uncomfortable
It's gonna move like the waves of the sea
But in the end You will be *'FREE'*
'My Queen I cannot fix You'
'You are not broken'
I can only promise that we are going to get uncomfortably
comfortable
You will cry and You will stumble
You will get angry and frustrated
You will unleash Emotions that You never knew were there
But You will get to know the biggest secret that not many
know
Yet You will Grow
In this Journey of Self Love
That the only secret to *'Living the Best Life'* and one that was
promised to You
'Lies Within You'

A Woman's Worth

'I Am a Strong Woman'
The Conductor of My Destiny
My body is Beautifully sculptured with the finest lines
The most curviest curves
Brown skin so soft
Lips of a Nubian Queen
Eyes Created to see
The Beauty of things
Yet at times I talk the talk
I even walk the walk
Still I often forget My Worth
Faking a Smile
A *'Hello Madam or Sir'*
Wear a mask with a white shirt and black skirt
Tell Myself *'I Love what I do'* when I'm not following my call
Then the words of someone else
Expecting Me to serve
Looking down at Me not seeing that behind this uniform is
'A Woman of Worth'
Creates anger within Me
Not at them but at Myself for not really seeing My Capabilities
As a Woman
As a Diamond
As a Healer
Bringing Me back to My Ancestors
Who endured so much pain and slavery
To serve those who continued to hurt them
Humiliate them
Imprison them
And even rape them
Does that mean that their scars have been embedded within
Me
For accepting a job just because I believe it to be *'EASY'*
No there is more than just that
Maybe a feeling that this *"Freedom"* won't last

Soul of A Woman

That I'll have to beg just so someone can see that I have what
it takes to Guide them
To bring them out of their own *'slave mentality'*
Or is it the fear that the past often brings that this Feeling is
here temporarily
On one side I feel Beautiful and Capable of doing anything I
put my Mind to
On the other this part of Me just Feels tired
Of saying *'YES'* like a prostitute
Reminding Myself *'it's ok because it's temporary and not
degrading'*
'It's only serving a few drinks'
That soon I'll be doing what I am truly meant to and will be
Living the Life *'I Am Destined for'*
'Let go My Child'
It's the language I hear as I express Myself and My thoughts so
Freely
'Do not worry about the HOW'
Instead of saying *'YES'* and working for less
Say *'YES I AM WORTHY of receiving more'*
And *'Let Go'* of the stress
'I Am not my Ancestors'
'I Am not what they see'
They are simply reflecting what I often forget still Lives inside
Me
Yet *'I Am Free'*
Consciously
Yet subconsciously there's a Child that Lives inside a Queen
that Lived inside another Queen that down my family chain
was a *'SLAVE'*
'I Am here to break that chain'
I refuse to break out with so many scars to Live the story
others were not Capable of
They felt trapped and conformed to society's expectations of
them and gave up on themselves and were labelled...
'Black'
'Single Mother'
'Never married'

Soul of A Woman

'In debt'
'Living from job to job just to pay bills'
Listening to this list gives them chills
Let me give them something to be Excited about
Being *"Black"* does not make me a slave
Being *"a single Mother"* does not make me needy
"Never married" does not mean I have issues
"Being in debt" does not make me poor
"Living from job to job" does not make me weak
These were the paths that my Creator so graciously chose for
Me
Some I Accepted and chose because they Felt Better for Me
Others were choices from My Own need to care for those I
Love
All of these were lessons that have made Me the *'Woman I
Am today'*
I would not change a single one because I have learnt
That the Power to Create the Life that I Deserve means I have
many options but mostly
I have Power and Freewill to ask for what *'I Am worth'*
Demand what was Promised to Me
'A life of Abundance Love and Freedom'

I Am Free2Embrace Me

The touch of sand playfully caressing Her soft feet
So warm yet so tender tantalising Her senses
Like a Child eager to run into the cold waves of the sea
She holds back Embracing the roaring warm wind
Wanting this moment to last
Mindfully gazing at the wonders of the sea
Breathing Freedom that had once been stolen from Her
[DEEP BREATH]
Grateful for Her Strength
She took Her Breath back
'Wait it's always been Hers'
Slowly wetting Her toes
Giggling like a Child new to the touch of the water
Discovering
Connecting
Allowing
All of this world is Hers to Discover
To Create
With every step Excitement builds within Her
Like a slow unexpected Satisfying Orgasm
Water Rising Sensually up towards Her knees
Her thighs
Her round buttocks
Caressing Her Femininity
Shyly Feeling the wetness between Her thighs
Connecting with the motion of the waves
Hands together in Prayer
Cupping the wet waves in Her Strong Creative hands
Big Smile of Gratitude
[SPLASH]
She Laughs Excitedly
Waives always wave fast then slow
Yet they never stop moving
Her Destiny awaits Mysteriously to those whose Life She
touches

Soul of A Woman

To those Intrigued by Her Aura
Wondering eyes follow Her
'Who is She'
'How does She do it'
'What gives Her Strength'
Many questions yet only one answer
One Story
One Life
One Hope
A million words
Keep watching
Keep listening
Keep following
Keep reading
Where She is going no one will ever know
A Journey with no Destination
'I Am that I Am'
'I Am Free2Embrace Me'

"When I stepped into my own Self Love, everything I desired was already mine. I simply needed to allow myself to receive"

Pen to Paper

Mindfully these words She utters Faithfully
Thoughts consume Her like a dark cloud of Light constantly
Once it's written it lingers as a Self-fulfilling prophecy
Then an Action brings destruction or brings Creativity
No one knows what thoughts invade Her Beautiful Mind so
Instantly
Be careful what You Focus on
Be wise what You Believe
Take a moment to ask Your Mind
'Is it true'
Hear the voice of Your subconscious
Hear the sound of a Happiness thief
As a Child She was a sponge of all the words She learnt
All the things Her parents said
'You're such a naughty girl' Her Mother said
'Stop crying little girl' Her friends would laugh
'Stop being weak' Her Brother teased
Words are so Powerful
Yet She absorbed them as the Truth from the ones She loved
the most
Now as an adult She's afraid to cry
Because She will be told She mustn't
Will be told She has to be Strong
And if She touches Her most intimate parts She's reminded
that She's naughty
So ashamed She's in Self blame
Knowing that She can do what She pleases
Yet subconsciously Her Mind tells Her She's not to cry
Cause no one will Love Her if She does
'Put on my Mask like my Mother does'
Holding back tears She pretends
With a lump on Her throat
Knot in Her stomach She stands
Appearing Strong even though Her Heart breaks
Every broken piece neglected of Love

Soul of A Woman

Disconnected from Her *"SELF"*
Journal in hand Her Feelings flow
Words so Effortlessly written
Those who read Her words are left in awe of Her Gift of Self-
expression
The Beautiful way She tells Her Story
From breakdown to Breakthrough
Freeing Her Mind
Strengthening Her Spirit
Igniting a Fire burning with flames to Her Truth
So vivid
So raw
So real
So Authentic
Her Mind is an open book
A Journey of depression to Self-expression of a Poet who
writes Her way to Freedom
Just like *Phillis Wheatley* who became the First African
American Woman in 1773 to publish a book of Poetry
Then *Maya Angelou* who as an African American Woman
made history as the first non-fiction bestseller writing Poetry
and reciting it so Wonderfully
Believing one day that She too will be remembered as a
Legend
They all had a Gift to share to the world
They were heard through their Authenticity of spoken word
An Inspiration to many
An example of Strength
Yet they Loved so Passionately and Expressed so Eloquently
'As I put Pen to Paper I inhale Love'
'I Exhale Freedom'
My tears no longer make me Feel weak
I have a voice
Through Poetry I will continue to speak
A True Love Story Never Ends...

Embracing and Expressing Your Feelings will set you FREE.

Free2Embraceme

How Can I Be Your Guide?

I have helped many women, from all walks of life, find their own *"Inner Strength"* and ignite this *"Strength"* to step into their *"Greatness"*. Mind, Body and Spirit, we are all connected. I have the ability to see your worth before you see it, your path before we even begin to work together. The Gift to see your vision before you do. I know your path is already laid out for You. All you need is someone who has been there, who walks this path unapologetically, yet is humble and always present. I cannot fix You, You are not broken. You are beautiful and created with the finest hands with a purpose to Love and spread Love.

How can I help You ignite this beauty within?

By transforming You into the beautiful butterfly that you are, with small steps that You can take easily and lovingly. Here is a list of how we can begin this path together. However, there is only one requirement, that you say *'YES I Am worthy'*:

I Love Myself Retreats

'Free2embrace Me Health & Wellbeing Movement'.

Women only day Retreats in London and Weekend Retreats in hot, sunny countries. Connect with Your Mind, Body and Spirit. *You will never walk this path alone once you become part of this movement.*

'Be Free to Eat What I Want' - **12 Week Transformational Coaching.** *This is my signature program for those wishing to free themselves from 'Body Perfection, Stop dieting and begin to eat what they want guilt-free'.*

'I am worthy of Loving Me' - **12 Week Transformational Coaching.** *'Step into Your Greatness and be Self Less'.*

'Feel the Fear and Do it Anyway' - **8 Week online Transformational Coaching.** *'Step into Your own BOSSness and Abundance'.*

Different coaching programmes tailor-made to you. You are not lost, you are being planted. Let's grow your roots and begin to Love You and Everything in Life and Business *'I Got You'.* These are available Face to Face by video call and online. It doesn't matter where you are in the world, we can still work together.

AWN - All Women's Network *Founder - Hannah Kupoluyi*

I am part of the All Women's Network as a Speaker and Mentor. If you are a woman in business, or wish to start a business, connect with us and be a part of Entrepreneurial women doing it together. *You will never be alone in business.*

APSC – Afro Portuguese Speaking Community in partnership – *Founder Osvaldo Gomes*

Working in partnership with the APSC team to support our Afro-Portuguese community, to aid inclusion and inspire them towards *"Change to become Leaders, Movers and Shakers".* Working with teen girls, women within our Women's Wellbeing Centre and providing Self Development work-shops/training/jobs/mentorship/entrepreneurship.

Speak or Host Your Event - Tailor-made speaking/hosting packages to make that occasion special. *'With a touch of class, a dust of Love a tingle to make You laugh a vision to Empower* *and Mission to Transform'.* When we raise our voices we shine together.

Events I have hosted are Mental Health, Women's support groups, business anniversaries, awards ceremonies, poetry nights, Women's breakfast meetings and Mastermind coaching workshops.

Train to gain Academy Founder William Kamara

Teacher & Assessor of Health & Wellbeing/Fitness courses – *Available on a freelance basis.*

21 Days to Calm Your Mind and Love Your Body Detox Fast Track System

'Be Free of Perfection mentality'

Ever wonder why some people change so quickly yet others take years, or even remain stuck?

Do you feel that this is impossible for you?

Do you believe you have to spend thousands of pounds to enrol on to a 1-month retreat and extreme total mind and body detox?

Although a lot of my programs take between 8-12 weeks for a person to transform, as we go through the different steps I mention in this book the transformation is instant.

Once you make a decision to embark on your own journey of self-love, you can achieve this in as little as 21 days as Your mind is so much clearer now that You're able to repeat the steps in every area of Your life, by listening to Your intuition, subconsciously.

What is the '21 Days to Calm Your Mind and Love Your Body Detox'?

It's a group coaching program delivered online via Face-book/whatsapp group. It combines all the steps I have listed in this book and it's provided daily. It guides you along with other beautiful souls on how to put these steps into place easily and effortlessly. It's like having your own accountability coach giving you *'EVERYTHING'* You need to get started in Your own *'Healing journey'* at Your own pace.

This remote program can be used by anyone no matter where you are in the world. Get in touch with me to find out more.

It's a start to begin creating your path and bringing mental, emotional, physical and spiritual cleanse in a gentle and easy way.

Guess what I throw in an extra week just to make sure you are fully supported.

About the Author

Neusa's strongest characteristics are that of a risk taker. A dreamer, one who speaks and follows through with action *'Less thinking more doing'* has always been Her Motto. This Strength, stubbornness and independence may not always feel good to those She Loves, as they often felt they had no place in Her life. She always knew from an early age to give to others.

Many failed, and still fail, to understand Her way of thinking; often pulling Her back to their own reality. Trapped in society's expectations of what a Mother should be. Seeing Her own Mother raise Her and Her three siblings alone gave Her the passion to repeat the same Strengths Her Queen Mother inherited from Her Grandmother and Her Ancestors.

Neusa Catoja, Born in Mozambique, Nampula on the 24th March 1979, moved to Portugal at the age of 3 with Her older Brother and single Mother. She watched Her own Mother struggle and work hard, just to provide for them all.

She faced many challenges as a child of a single parent: having little memories of Her childhood apart from the responsibilities of raising Her Younger Brother as Her Mother continued to work endlessly.

Moving to England at the age of 10, Neusa learned to speak English yet maintained Her own first language, Her African heritage; and still adapted to the English ways: cold weather and at times, friends who had no family values or respect for their parents.

At the age of 18 She left home to finally begin Her own journey of independence. Growing up in an African household, where girls cannot do what boys can, Her Mother did the best She could. However She craved Freedom and to just to be a normal teenager: to party hard, work hard and live Her own life without rules. Yes Neusa does not do rules of any kind.

Following a career as a 9-5 Personal Assistant, She was bored of the endless daily repetitive tasks that the corporate world restricted Her with.

She loved being a Mother, spending the majority of Her parenthood as a single Mother, as She craved Freedom and self-expression. At times She felt restricted in relationships; not because of Her partners, but because She had a desire to be Free. Feeling there was more to life than what was apparent.

The desire to be *"Great"* always lived within Her. She broke free as a fully qualified Personal Trainer, Entrepreneur, Mumpreneur. Friends often forgot She had a child. Not because She wasn't present in Her daughter's life but because having a child never restricted Her; It motivated Her to Love more, Do more and still enjoy life as a young mum.

Life was always on Her terms until one day Her risk taking began to take its toll.

Being Her own *"EVERYTHING"* became Her weakness, yet Her Greatest Strength. A Journey of Self Discovery led Her down a dark path of Body Dysmorphia; Depression and Social Anxiety. She experienced Emotional Eating; Binge Eating Disorder; Orthorexia; Obsession with Body Perfection; Self-harm; and suicidal thoughts; which led to a path of Discovery of *"SELF"*, igniting the fire within.

This path became Her awakening. Her obsession and addiction to the internet: searching for a solution to heal Her anxious thoughts, physical and self-diagnosed medical issues holistically led Her to become Her own Coach.

Her connection to Her Higher Power, the Goddess within Her led Her towards a relationship with God, Her Creator. Through this Spiritual connection Free2Embrace Me was born.

As a Certified Neuro Linguistic Programmer, Life Coach, Public Speaker, Teacher/Assessor/Mentor, Holistic Medical Community Tutor, Poet, Public Speaker, Host, Founder of 'I Love Myself First Retreats', Creator of 'Afrokiz Movement' and Holistic Free Spirit: over the past 8 years - which included Her own Self-Healing Journey - She is equipped to guide women who suffer with the *"Perfection Mentality"* to break free and unleash their own inner *"Gifts"*, to help them to *"Create"* and make a difference to others.

One vision to *"Empower Women"* connects other beautiful amazing women seeing and discovering their own *"Worth"* and taking a stand to be seen and heard resulting in taking their *"Power Back".*

Soul of A Woman

I Am is the most powerful word we use.

As I used my words I became whatever I said 'I AM'

I Am the Soul that You Breathe
I Am the Light that Shines within
I Am the friend that You Desire
I Am the Woman who will Inspire
I Am so pure
I Am of Worth
I Am Awakened Spiritually
I Am a Guide who is Sincere
I Am a Protector
I Am a Mother
I Am a Queen of Hearts
I Am My words
I Am My thoughts
I Am the cause

I made a Choice to Speak 'I Am' into Existence
I Am here to make a difference
I Am a Nurturer by Nature
A Provider by Experience
A Lover by default
A Healer by Strength

Affected by others behaviours at times confused by my own
fears of what is expected of Me as a Mother
I Smile at the world
When it Feels so overwhelming and I Feel the world on my
shoulders
The tightening of the S on my chest Breathes hard for rest
For someone to take me in their arms and say *'it's ok not to be
ok'*
'It's ok to ask for help'
Or a simple *'I got You'*
What You see is a cape

Soul of A Woman

A Wonderwoman
Who suffers emotionally
Expresses physically and still inspires others vocally
I Am not a superhero
I Am covered by scars
Protected by Angels
And Guided by my Creator
'I Am a Woman of Worth'

Printed in Poland
by Amazon Fulfillment
Poland Sp. z o.o., Wrocław